REVEALING
THE MISSING
Peace

JANE M POWERS

Revealing the Missing Peace is a must-read for anyone that has suffered abuse. It's also a must for anyone in a relationship with someone that has suffered abuse. With clarity, Jane M Powers leads readers to understand they are not alone in their search for peace and gives easy to follow options to heal the residual effects. Her transparency is beautiful. Adding to the power of the book is the addition of Denise's story. Different stories with similar outcomes allow readers to open their minds to how their personal stories are unique, but the solutions are universal. A brilliant piece of work!

— LAUREN ARCHIBEQUE,
Owner of The Growth Company USA and
bestselling author of *Be Nice and Get What You Really Want*

Packed with riveting real-life stories, "Reveal the Missing Peace" is essential reading for anyone who has experienced sexual abuse... or really any abuse. Jane goes deep, sharing personal gut-wrenching experiences that moves the reader through the value of vulnerability into the courageous steps they can take to create their own peace. Buy your copy today!

— DEBORAH DUBREE,
Elite Performance Expert and author
of *AVERAGE IS AN ADDICTION, From Mediocre to Millions!*

By tearing down the norms about addressing sexual abuse, Jane M. Powers has written a must-read primer. Her "tell it like it is" style is incredibly engaging, and her advice is loving, heartfelt, and sometimes includes a big kick in the pants, all with the aim of enabling readers to reveal their missing peace and empower themselves. Jane's big heart, raw and beautiful stories, and practical but powerful tips combine into an intense elixir for the soul. Read this book - and learn from one of the best.

— KIM ELEY,
Writing Coach and Publishing Consultant at KWE Publishing

What Jane M Powers has done in *Revealing the Missing Peace* is nothing short of a miracle. With honesty, understanding and intention, she takes a bold stand for those who have experienced the unimaginable in life. In classic style, Jane blends story and teaching, anecdotes with hard truths, all with the goal of helping you find the peace you deserve. Unless we heal our pain, we will not soar, and with Jane's step-by-step guidance, you get that much closer to living your life of freedom.

— LINDA ALBRIGHT, Women's Wealth Revolution

What a powerful book! After sharing her story, I found myself feeling "seen" in a way I hadn't before. This book is a must-read for anyone looking to remove the obstacles that are holding them back. What is holding you back from that new career? Position? Client? Relationship? Move? Using her unique blend of incredible expertise and relatable storytelling, Jane serves up a dose of reality that will shake you out of that rut and place you decidedly on a path where you control your life. She gives easy to apply strategies for creating the best version of yourself using gratitude, visioning, and the power of a vivid imagination. She will make you laugh, cry, and believe in yourself more than you ever thought possible. We have all lived a life...it is time to truly live.

— STEVIE DAWN CARTER, Stevie Dawn Inspires, LLC

Wow! Getting introduced to the gut-wrenching world of abuse is both eye opening and tragic. It's unimaginable how many people are affected either personally or through someone they know. The book starts out giving you a rather hopeless view of the world and some of its cruel inhabitants. But the steps described to help you find your PEACE are absolutely transformational. Although much work is required, it's definitely worth the time spent to find yourself amongst the outside forces that have ruled a life or past riddled with abuse. Going down the difficult journey to finding your PEACE, includes what must be one of the most difficult steps: Conquering Forgiveness. But what an important step that Jane outlines in the book.

If you have the desire to know more about the challenges of living through abuse, have an acquaintance who experienced abuse, or you were abused personally, this book is a must read!

— S. PAUL MOEHRING,
Business Coach, Speaker, Author of *Get Squared:
Goal Getting with Balance*

When would I find a way out of the darkness and give way to the silent scream? I had a longing for a better life, a safer life, a freer life – a life of Peace," writes Jane M. Powers in her powerful book *Revealing the Missing Peace*; a story of bravery, survival, and a guide for women of sexual abuse to step confidently into a brighter future. From victim to vanquisher, Powers' personal abuse experiences, knowledge, and advice expose the strength of our mind, to both heal and hurt, and shows women how to redefine a new truth and a new life as a "Surviv*OR*." Gripping and brilliant!

— JANE APPLEGATH, Creative Intelligence Coach

Revealing The Missing Peace brought such mixed emotions, I just could not put it down. My first reaction was anger that Jane, Denise, or anyone had to go through such ordeals, hmmmm, that is not even the appropriate word to apply, is it?

I have hidden myself from my past for decades, never really wanting to know why the things in my childhood occurred, fearful of what I would remember. Sexual abuse was not my situation. As revealed in this book, there are many different types of abuse and we must recognize those that have shaped us.

As I continued through each chapter, my awareness grew as to the importance of reflecting, recognizing, and realizing the paths and choices that were before me.

The knowledge contained within these pages is beneficial to all readers. The wisdom is pivotal in the opportunity to Reveal The Missing Peace that I avoided all my life.

This is a must read to move from survivor to surviOR.

— EILEEN GALBRAITH,
Credit Knowhow, LLC

So many times, we go through life searching for something. We're never quite sure what it is and yet we continue to search. As women, we search for the words and for our voices to shed light on that missing piece. In her book, *Revealing The Missing Peace*, Jane M Powers helps you discover what that missing piece is to give you that missing peace. This book is on my nightstand so that it is handy to refer and to and reminds me to reclaim that missing peace I finally understand.

— JUDY HOBERMAN,
President, Selling In A Skirt

After seeing Jane completely transform people from the stage in front of a crowd of hundreds, I'm not surprised she figured out how to put that candor, wit, and wisdom passionately into a book.

The words leap out at you from page one like you're watching a movie with her, her wife, and many others' stories of being abused in many different ways (and on many different levels) making the reader feel like he/she is part of a friendly inner circle. She then rolls it all up into an intellectual system that breaks down the simple steps to heal and move forward in a way that feels like she is taking your hand by gently explaining and consequently inspiring you the entire way.

— JUDY GOSS,
TV Personality, Emcee, Speaker,
Author of *Break Into Modeling for $20*

This book is a must read if you've experienced abuse and want to get to the other side of it. Jane's display of resiliency and commitment to claim her life back is very impressive. She's been through the fire and is thriving, successful, and happy. She peels the layers away that are the result of abuse and gives the tools and a course of action to claim the life that is waiting for you.

— WANDA ALLEN,
Follow Up Expert at Follow Up Strategies

In *Revealing the Missing Peace,* Jane M Powers shares the real and raw truth about her past of abuse, how she overcame it, and how you can also. In a first-hand and powerful way, Jane will take you step-by-step through realizing your truth, speaking your truth, taking your life back, and creating the best new reality imaginable. If you are looking to connect to your truth, if you are looking to rise above your past, if you are ready to create a new story and a new life, I highly recommend this book.

— JENNY HARKLEROAD,
founder of Balanced You™ and one of Jane M Power's biggest fans!!!

Jane shares her personal story of abuse and recovery and offers you the thoughts, questions, and actions that can make a difference in your life. In her search for peace, she found there is nothing missing. Her belief is that we have everything we need to feel and live in peace and she shares the steps to help you find your peace. It is an amazing way to look at going forward and gives hope, comfort and support to every reader.

She gives insight into the concept of Power and Control and the vulnerability it creates in life. She shares how triggers impact lives and how to overcome the feelings of being a victim.

In telling her story, she shares that the greatest power for recovery is finding your voice. She takes you down her unique path to finding her voice and gives suggestions and guidance for every step in the process.

Jane uses her story and journey to help guide you down the path to the peace you deserve to have. She provides education, suggestions, and tools to help you achieve a new reality.

I recommend this book to anyone who is recovering from abuse and anyone who has a loved one that is facing this challenge. Whether you are on the path to recovery or don't know how or where to start, her guidance and suggestions are life changing.

— CAROLYN ANDREWS, Inspired Leaders Now

So many times in my life, dealing with trauma means digging into it. Remembering and reliving all the details. At some point, it becomes a tradeoff. I want to heal, but I dread the process. And then I read this book. Finally, a method that works without me having to go into the darkness again, alone. This book is opening up a new world for me. Thank you, Jane!

— RJ REDDEN, Black Belt Bots

REVEALING THE MISSING Peace

JANE M POWERS

Spotlight
PUBLISHING

Goodyear, AZ

ISBN:978-1-953806-39-0 Paperback Book
ISBN: 978-1-953806-40-6 eBook
Library of Congress Control Number: 2021910013

Editor: Kimberly Eley - KWE Publishing
Cover Art: Crystal Cregge – www.lionadesignco.com
Photography by: Jane M Powers
Interior Layout: Amit Dey
Publisher: Spotlight Publishing™ www.spotlightpublishing.pro

Disclaimer: I am not a psychologist, psychiatrist, Master of Social Work (MSW), Licensed Social Worker (LSW), nor am I a therapist. ALL INFORMATION CONTAINED in this book and e-book is intended for your general knowledge only and is not a substitute for advice or treatment. I cannot and do not give professional advice. If you have specific questions about any matters, you should consult a qualified professional provider.

Jane M Powers
www.JaneMPowers.com
www.RevealingTheMissingPeace.com
Jane@janempowers.com

Table of Contents

Foreword

When asked which moments define us, we usually answer by sharing positive events. We might think back on achievements, graduations, victories, and celebrations with families and friends. What we often keep from sharing are the trying times, the moments when we failed, and the days when we were afraid, anxious, or uncertain. Yet when we look at the moments that made us who we really are, the difficulties and challenges are the ones that stand out. We are defined in many ways by what we have faced and overcome.

As a writer and speaker for over twenty years and as a blind person, I love a great story about facing challenges. Storytelling involves being vulnerable, engaging your readers, and leading them on a new path. As readers, we place our trust in the author to take us to a place where we may not have been.

When Jane M. Powers writes, she understands her responsibility as a writer, and she takes care of her readers. A writer and speaker herself, she utilizes the power of a story. She understands how stories and our interpretation of their meaning can transform us. When she approached me about writing the foreword to this book, she shared her story of sexual abuse and learning to be a survivor, not a victim. That message resonated with me for several reasons.

First, the courage that we, as the visually impaired, have to face each day, along with its challenges, are ironically something others can see. You can witness someone using a cane or reading Braille. The bravery of people who have survived sexual abuse is hidden, however, and not in plain sight. And yet, what these two challenges have in common is that both require one to have the courage to adopt a different mindset, an inner strength to do the things that are difficult not just to survive but to thrive.

I learned through research that there is a correlation between people who are visually impaired and people who have been sexually abused. People with visual impairments have a greater risk of experiencing sexual assault than the general population. Sexual assault is largely about power and oppression. In light of this fact, I especially wanted to commend Ms. Powers for her message and mission. In her "tell it like it is" manner, she acknowledges there will be challenges, but she shows that her readers can reclaim their strength.

Ms. Powers gives back power to those who might feel powerless through her frank and open verbiage. She talks openly about abusers and exposes them for who they are. Her humor and engaging way of writing make the reader feel at ease and lets them know they are taking this journey with a trusted friend. Having worked with others in recovery, Ms. Powers knows her stuff. She also has the courage of her convictions, taking an unconventional approach to therapy.

While I appreciate the entire book, the section about "The Dark Night" particularly resonates with me. How we react to the moments in our lives where we face our doubts, where we walk up to the pain, walk around in it, and then carry on with our lives. Having addressed it is crucial, and a step others want to avoid. It takes real grit to face your greatest pain, and it takes a lot of trust. Ms. Powers makes real, effective changes with her readers by being willing to go to the hard places and face the truth.

I know that when you read Ms. Powers' book, you are opening yourself up, declaring that you are ready to embrace peace in your life, and are ready to reveal the missing peace you deserve. Get ready for this journey and to change your life.

Jim Stovall

www.jimstovall.com

Introduction:

I knew something wasn't right. Prior to meeting Jane M. Powers, however, I just dismissed it. Proudly declaring myself to be "Daddy's special girl," I loved my relationship with my father. Sure, there was friction between me and my mother, but outwardly we were the perfect family.

As an adult, I was a constant people pleaser with no idea where that motivation came from. Growing up, without seeking their attention, older men would flock to me. It was as though I had a beacon that was invisible to me that drew the wrong people my way.

Jane and I have been working together for four years. During that time, for the first time, I had made peace with the uneasiness that robbed my sense of well-being. With her *Revealing the Missing Peace* methodology, I learned I had been sleepwalking through my life. My mind was unconsciously shielding me from getting too close to others and simultaneously attracting unwanted attention.

What I had cherished as special treatment from my father was revealed to me later as grooming me to be his dependent. For years, I doted on him, feeling that I was the best person to care for his physical ailments and even rescue his failing business. I had convinced myself that his intentions were always for the highest good. This mindset made it incredibly difficult to face the fact that I had been abused. How could someone I respected and put on a pedestal have had anything but pure motives?

Abusers intentionally mislead their victims and use their feelings of shame and guilt to control them. What makes this especially devastating is that we as survivors continue to utilize the patterns of control that we have been taught. Simply put, we live by what we know. In my case, since I felt obligated to care for my father and felt I was the only person who could, my mindset spilled over into every aspect of my life. I could not say 'no' to helping people, even at the risk of not attending to my own needs. This made me put myself on the back burner in all of my relationships. As you will learn, I became not only mentally numb but physically, too. My mind enabled me to zone out to protect myself as I walked through the world with the damaged programming I was taught.

The worst part was that I was unhappy and I had no idea why. I told other people the story of coming from a perfect family. I bought into the illusion that I was my father's favorite because I was special. And because I was considered special, I believed I had obligations beyond my boundaries. Heck, I didn't even believe I could have boundaries. The programming ran deep.

What I benefited most from Jane's *Revealing the Missing Peace* program was her gentle and unconventional approach. Traditional therapy derives its approach from its focus on the memories from the abuse and its impact on your personality. The belief for years has been that you must open your subconscious mind and access the vault of memories within in order to heal. While this method can be effective, in some instances it can also cause a great deal of damage. As survivors, our minds have purposefully kept certain events blocked from us as a means of protection. Opening this "vault" too soon or when we are not ready can have devastating consequences.

With *Revealing the Missing Peace,* Jane states you can indeed face your abuser, and their impact on you, without having to relive every moment of the abuse. You will still have a powerful, meaningful recovery. Jane and I share our different approaches to our abuse in this book to empower you. All along, we offer options for addressing the abuse, and provide straight talk on what works and why.

You will find that Jane talks openly and frankly about her abuse and healing journey. Those of you who are already familiar with her incredible presence on speaking stages will recognize her delightful humor and her "tell it like it is" style. I am proud of her for going to these difficult places.

Jane's way of describing this revolutionary program boils down to a choice. Do you want to survive, or do you want to be a suriv*OR?* As you read the upcoming pages, I want to let you know Jane and I are holding space for you. You are making a deliberate choice to not just survive, but to open yourself up to your best possible life. Choosing to feel again, to take back the control that was stolen from you, and to do the difficult work is so brave. We are so proud of you as you begin to do this work.

You may be thinking, *I'm not an abuse survivor. What will I learn?* While the intended audience for *Revealing the Missing Peace* is primarily victims of abuse, we have heard from others who have not experienced abuse who have beneficially applied her advice and techniques to their lives. I'm so glad this book and its message has even more reach than we had intended.

My hope for you is to continue moving forward and doing well! We welcome you to become a fellow surviv*OR.*

Denise Romano Powers

Preface

*N*ight falls, and darkness begins to take over the once sun-filled room. The all-too-familiar silence fills the air, a silence filled with expectation and fear. It is a night like all other nights I have grown accustomed to but have been destined never to understand. I live each day in fear of the darkness because there is a ritual–a selection if you will–that always ends in pain. There is no sense in fighting, hoping, or praying for something different.

I grew up knowing how the family system worked. It was a never-ending routine, a pattern, an existence that engulfed me in confusion, terror, shame, and dread. When would it all end? When would I find a way out of the darkness and give way to the silent scream? I always had a longing for a better life, a safer life, a freer life–a life of PEACE.

My Story

My story began before I had words that could define what was happening. I, like many, lived in a world of secrets. No one knew these dark secrets and the suffering I held deep inside from my abuse. I was a master at playing the role of the average kid with a wonderful family. I smiled all the time to ensure my secret was safe. In the lead roles of student, athlete, helper, and best friend, my life was a play, and I was the star. I knew what to say, what not to say, and how to honor the family secret.

But my world was a lonely place of silence and suffering. I believed God forgot me. I could not imagine a God who would allow anything as horrible as my life to happen to a small child. If God remembered me, I thought, there would be no way this suffering would have occurred.

There was a part of me that knew my life was not to be this way. At the age of fourteen, a fight deep in my soul began to give birth to hope and possibility. I had no frame of reference for freedom or peace, but I felt I was a survivor, despite not totally understanding what that even meant. I was wired to overcome this part of my life and one day make a difference for others. No matter the pain or the amount of suffering I endured, I would one day free myself from the bondage of my abuse. I was determined to find a way to be free from a life of shame, guilt, and self-blame. I was destined to break out of my silence and free the reality buried deep inside of me–the TRUTH. The truth of who I am and what I can create in my life. I knew there was more love, more joy–more peace.

My Voice

Finding my voice and breaking the silence were the first steps in a very long journey of healing. Writing this book is my way of empowering and supporting others who have already walked or are walking a similar path. My journey through the dark night of the soul into the light of my dream was long and often very lonely.

As long as we identify ourselves as a survivor, we remain tied to our abuse. What if you can change the past and how it affects your present and future? *Revealing the Missing Peace* guides those on a healing journey from the pain of abuse who want to transform and be a surviv*OR*. It's your choice. Do you survive, *OR*? When you choose *OR*, you choose to live more than survive. I hope you allow yourself to gain knowledge, insights, and tools to live an *OR* life.

I will walk you through the surviv*OR* process to transform your life as you know it. Be warned: This is not for those who lack courage, commitment, dedication, willpower, inspiration, desperation, or are lazy. Growth and healing require keeping your eye on the prize–an *OR* life.

What is an *OR* life? My definition is anchored in the freedom to have a life beyond merely surviving. As a survivor, part of you always lives in the past. You can't help it; I can't help it. Abuse of any degree and kind creates who you are. The way you react, feel, cower, fight, struggle, strive, drive, or quit is designed by your past. I intend to prove to you that you are more than your history and you are far more than what happened to you.

Each time someone says, "I am a survivor," they are claiming their past. Let's claim that the past is over and redesign a future of an *OR*–or better yet, let's declare a "YES AND"– life now.

Team Powers

The mission, if you choose to accept it, is to reveal your missing *peace* and *piece*. I have invited Denise M. Powers to support me on this mission because Denise has been working with me for over four years, revealing her peace and piece. She is the perfect participant to walk through the healing in this book, step by step, page by page.

Denise and I could not be more opposite in our personalities, processes, and outlooks.

This is excellent as you, the reader, compare our stories side-by-side. You have the best of both worlds. We intend to offer you a full perspective as you go through your process. Denise and many, many others have embraced my techniques and strategies. I wanted to bring her into the book for our blended experiences to benefit you more profoundly.

So, here we go!

CHAPTER 1

Stand for Peace

Nobel Peace Prize
Peace Movement
Peace Treaties
Peace Corps
World Peace
Prince of Peace
War and Peace
Give Peace A Chance

And–the ever-popular "Peace Be With You," my auto-response at church growing up.

Peace is one of the greatest desires amongst most people. There are numerous movements, organizations, movies, songs, and sayings that express the vision of global peace.

So, what is peace? As survivors of sexual abuse, we have battled to have peace our entire lives. We are wrestling day in and day out to feel whole or, at minimum, ordinary. As a survivor, you are a master at looking great on the outside.

However, inside of us, there is a never-ending, nagging feeling like something is missing. In our search to find the *piece*, we fill this void with people, places, and things, including vices such as food, chemicals, sex, gambling, shopping, and co-dependence. Every bit of effort to find this piece is a quest to achieve our ultimate goal–*peace*.

As a survivor of sexual abuse, I believed for years if I could find the missing *PIECE* within me, I would find my missing *PEACE!* I set out on this peace journey in 1985 after putting my fist through a dorm room window. I was struggling with inner and outer turmoil because domestic violence riddled my relationship. My greatest desire was *peace*, which at that time felt unattainable. If there was peace in the world, I believed I was not one of the lucky ones to live it. After over 36 years of searching, you will not believe what I discovered–there is NO missing *PIECE*, let alone missing *PEACE*!!!

What?! I lived my entire life searching for what was there all the time. Nothing is missing! We have everything we need to feel and live in peace. Now, if that is the case, why do so many feel the void of both piece and peace in their lives? That's what we will address in *Revealing Your Missing Peace*.

I am starting our movement: *Revealing Your Missing Peace*. My goal is to help you begin to understand your perspective or definition of your inner peace. Because you are here, I am going to assume you have the same desire for peace.

Before we get going, I want to make it crystal clear that any level of abuse is ABUSE. The measurement of abuse is more than the degree of violation, penetration or not, verbal or physical, number of times, or age; it is the degree of feeling it activates within you. In this book, we will dive into the activation of triggers and running life on autopilot. First, let's look at abuse and how it can highjack your life without you even knowing.

Trust me, my most incredible fight in life was to maintain ultimate control. Despite the outward appearance, my life was insanely out of control, and I could not continue allowing it. Abuse has a way of causing one to feel crazy, or at least that is how I felt. I questioned my reality and "what was wrong with me." Something was just not right. I felt like I was out of my body on many days, and on others, I just wanted to be out of my body. It was a vicious cycle. I refer to my early years as my pre-memory life. Each day was a mystery of why I was so emotionally distraught and suffering in silence.

Abuse is the *gift* that keeps on giving, no matter what form. Since beginning my healing journey in 1985 I have discovered that each event in my life leads to the next opportunity to reveal more of the missing PEACE. Do not step into comparanoia, which means to compare yourself to others, unrealistically.

For example, when I would share my story with a group of survivors, others would discount their abuse. They began comparing their past with mine, and since they didn't perceive theirs to be as bad, they would minimize their reactions and actions around their experiences of abuse. Stop! There is no comparing or *One-Upping* in the world of abuse. How does one *One-Up?*

It is the process of outdoing another. I have experienced this many times in conversations. If I shared that my abuse occurred three to four times a week, some people would say, "Oh, that's nothing, you should hear my story," or, "I can top that." Trust me. I would give anything to have a story perceived as *not so bad*.

The act of *One-Upping* is for the sole reason of being validated. It's a cry to be heard. Whenever someone is experiencing *comparanoia* or is *One-Upping* me, I immediately give them the attention they are seeking. I used to feel offended or annoyed because I believed I needed the attention. I was in pain and wanted someone to acknowledge how awful my experiences were growing up. At that point, I was blind to the fact that others needed attention as much as I did.

I highly recommend you find one confidante to share your experiences with as you go through the healing process. Get permission from this trusted person to share any and all feelings and experiences. You want to remove guesswork, so give the person direction on how to support you. For example, you may prefer the person to hug you or verbally acknowledge you. This communication will set up both of you for success.

Now, let's look at abuse, the effects, memories, and you. Since you are reading this book, you know about some forms of abuse already. You understand that any form of abuse is a corrupt practice or custom, improper or excessive use or treatment of a person or thing, whether emotional, verbal, physical, or sexual. Abuse can include the act of bullying, manipulating, condemning, humiliating, deceiving, tricking, neglecting, beating, spanking, and more.

There are said to be five essential types of child abuse:

1. **Emotional abuse** is a chronic pattern of behavior such as belittling, humiliating, and ridiculing a child.
2. **Emotional neglect** is the consistent inability of parents or caretakers to provide a child with appropriate support, attention, and affection.
3. **Physical neglect** is the failure to provide children with adequate food, clothing, shelter, and medical care. Physical neglect also includes abandonment, expulsion

from home, and failure to enroll children in school. It is essential to distinguish between willful neglect and a parent's inability to provide life necessities because of poverty and cultural norms.

4. ***Physical abuse*** includes acts of physical assault by parents, caretakers, or strangers. Physical abuse includes cuts, fractures, bruises, shaking, burns, and internal injuries.

5. ***Sexual abuse*** includes acts of sexual assault and sexual exploitation of minors by parents, caregivers, or strangers. It may consist of a single incident or many incidents over a long time. It includes fondling a child's genitals, intercourse, incest, rape, sodomy, exhibitionism, and sexual exploitation.

I believe there are numerous types of abuse, and I recognize these are not limited to children. As adults, many of us have experienced sexual assault, domestic violence, discrimination, and cultural, financial, and psychological abuse. I know I have.

Studies and surveys estimate that sexual abuse occurs before eighteen for one in three girls and one in six boys. Incest occurs at similar rates across all social classes. As you may have guessed, ninety percent of child sexual abuse victims know their perpetrator, and sixty-eight percent are abused by a family member. I will focus on the healing and transformation in this book.

For abuse data, visit to learn more:

http://www.d2l.org/wpcontent/uploads/2017/01/all_statistics_20150619.pdf

If you are a statistic, you have come to the right place. As they say, knowledge is power, and this power ignites change. Unfortunately, once abused, always abused.

Hold on–allow me to explain. When I said, "Once abused, always abused," I am not saying you will experience abuse in the same way as in the past. What I am saying is that you are prone to it in one form or another. Abuse sets up a pattern or program in your system–also known as how you function–resulting in more abuse throughout your life by oneself or others. How?

Our grooming, training, conditioning, upbringing, and programming was for being controlled by another. An exception is a violent act of abuse, which is an outright assertion of control and power.

PHYSICAL VIOLENCE SEXUAL

POWER AND CONTROL

USING COERCION AND THREATS
Making and/or carrying out threats to do something to hurt her • threatening to leave her, to commit suicide, to report her to welfare • making her drop charges • making her do illegal things.

USING INTIMIDATION
Making her afraid by using looks, actions, gestures • smashing things • destroying her property • abusing pets • displaying weapons.

USING ECONOMIC ABUSE
Preventing her from getting or keeping a job • making her ask for money • giving her an allowance • taking her money • not letting her know about or have access to family income.

USING EMOTIONAL ABUSE
Putting her down • making her feel bad about herself • calling her names • making her think she's crazy • playing mind games • humiliating her • making her feel guilty.

USING MALE PRIVILEGE
Treating her like a servant • making all the big decisions • acting like the "master of the castle" • being the one to define men's and women's roles

USING ISOLATION
Controlling what she does, who she sees and talks to, what she reads, where she goes • limiting her outside involvement • using jealousy to justify actions.

USING CHILDREN
Making her feel guilty about the children • using the children to relay messages • using visitation to harass her • threatening to take the children away.

MINIMIZING, DENYING AND BLAMING
Making light of the abuse and not taking her concerns about it seriously • saying the abuse didn't happen • shifting responsibility for abusive behavior • saying she caused it.

PHYSICAL VIOLENCE SEXUAL

Let's learn more about how we might have fallen under the spell of control by looking at the Power and Control Wheel developed by the National Center for Domestic and Sexual Violence.[1]

The Power and Control Wheel is a tool that allows you to sort out the "crazy-making" behavior you may have experienced throughout the time of your abuse and in your life. Whether it was one time or for a lifetime, you were on this wheel at some point.

I am going to take the liberty of interpreting the Power and Control Wheel in my own words. Power and control are in the center of the wheel because they are at the center of the abuse. A perpetrator systematically uses threats, intimidation, and coercion to instill fear to perpetrate the act of abuse. These behaviors are the spokes of the wheel. Physical and sexual violence holds it all together–this violence is the rim of the wheel.

Please know that the purpose of sharing stories in this book is to serve you, the reader, and support you in your transformation and understanding the terms on the Power and Control Wheel.

Dominance: Abusive individuals needed to feel in charge of the relationship. They made decisions for you and others, told you what to do, and expected you to obey without question. Your abuser may have treated you like a servant, hostage, or even his/her possession. Alternatively, abusers are crafty, as they can persuade with charm, care, and support. Another method they use to manipulate is enrolling you in being of service or placating the abuser. In other words, you are convinced that you are their saving grace and that your outstanding care for them is imperative in improving their lives; they depend on you to be truly happy.

Jane's Story of Dominance: Growing up as the youngest of seven kids, I observed our family's hierarchy. No one questioned my father about anything. He led with soundless intimidation and had very few overt acts of anger or outburst, yet somehow his silently controlling demeanor was enough to keep us in line. I followed the proper protocol of my family and was very intimidated by my father and other abusers.

In the era in which I grew up, children and women gave all the power to the male figure at home. They were assumed to be the smartest and most powerful. Ironically, I forever felt like a dummy. I imagine being told I was dumb and stupid by my father contributed to that belief. While I was attending college, I asked my father what his grade point average (GPA) was when he attended the University of Wisconsin, Madison. He confessed he was an average "C" student. WHAT?! I could not believe it. I had a 4.0 GPA, yet he called me stupid. How was I convinced he was the superior being at all things? Dominance worked!

My father displayed emotional dominance while the others in my family acted with physical authority. Many times, I was dragged down the hall into the bedroom by my brother. Using one hand to act as a handcuff around my wrists, I was held down, pinned, choked, and sat on to assert his power over me. If I struggled or resisted, the physical consequences became exponentially worse. I was little but I was determined, yet to no avail.

You may wonder, why the heck don't we fight more against our abusers? We don't because our training was to either behave or cooperate through manipulation. As children, none of us had the means to reason out the circumstances. These areas of brain development don't occur until much later. It is easy as an adult to walk through what you would do since you are older, and your brain understands actions have consequences. Heck, as a kid, you had to touch the hot stove to learn that son of a gun is HOT. You did not have the cognitive ability to string together the acts and future effects at that time. They told you to respect your elders, authority figures, and parents, so you did.

Denise's Story of Dominance: Earlier, I mentioned that some abusers manipulate with charm, kindness, and making you feel needed. This approach is what happened in Denise's experience. To this very day, she still has a challenging time with being angry at her father, despite what she now knows. Her father had numerous physical issues and spent most of his life in pain. As the eldest and the only girl, Denise was his special girl into adulthood. She would do anything to help him and felt responsible for his happiness.

While Denise doesn't recall any domination like my experience, her father manipulated her into feeling obligated. This type of dominance is genuinely a mind-bender. The charm, wit, kindness, and special treatment left her victim to a sense of obligation and unrecognized control.

The false sense of knowing she could contribute to his happiness made her feel good inside yet left her with an unconscious and misdirected sense of love and care. Being "daddy's special girl" felt like the best part, while later in life, she was triggered and repeated the pattern of caregiving to the world.

Dominance can show up in many ways. No matter the form, it has the same result and lasting effects.

Humiliation: An abuser did everything they could to make us feel bad about ourselves or somehow defective. No wonder we go through life questioning our value, worthiness, and deservedness. After all, if we believed we were worthless, we were more susceptible to advances, inappropriate or not. Insults, name-calling, shaming, and public put-downs were all weapons of abuse designed to erode our self-esteem and make us feel powerless. Humiliation can come from several enabling sources, not only the abuser.

Jane's Story of Humiliation: One of my brothers in particular was a master at humiliation. He would embarrass me in front of my siblings after he left his "mark." I would run to the bathroom to clean up and felt awful about myself. I was humiliated and ashamed. He would leave me a mess, belittle me, and call me names. His assertion of power was a means to make him feel better about himself.

Denise's Story of Humiliation: Ironically, Denise's humiliation didn't come from her father. He never made her feel less than or unworthy of anything. Instead, the shame Denise felt came from her mother. As she looks back, she now understands why her mother reacted toward her the way she did.

The reaction from other family members when there is abuse going on can vary. For Denise, her mother put her down whenever she didn't do something just right, and nothing was ever good enough. There was always room to do better, do more, and be greater than she was. Denise's mother made her feel unworthy of her attention, and thus she turned to her father for comfort.

Do you see the ultimate manipulation here? Her mother's reactions to what was happening made things worse and kept Denise in a state of desire for her father's positive attention.

Isolation: To increase your dependence on them, an abuser cuts you off from the outside world. They may have kept you from seeing family and friends, or even prevented you from participating in school functions, sports, parties, or other activities that could potentially expose you to confidants. You may have had to ask permission from them to do anything, go anywhere, or see anyone.

Jane's Story of Isolation: My training from birth ensured my obedience. I was never isolated from others, but I knew to keep the family secret. When with people outside of my family, I knew better than to say anything to anyone about my home life. Since my controlling father was confident I would keep the family secret, he gave me the freedom to go out and participate in activities.

I also believe he could convince himself he was doing nothing wrong. While I am not a Ph.D., I understand that my father had a dissociative disorder which allowed him to be *outside of himself* to abuse me. As a result, I was free to do whatever I wanted to do because he was "disconnected" from my abuse.

Having this freedom was perfect because it allowed me to participate in sports. As I lived to play any sport, I thank goodness I was a natural athlete. I excelled and honestly believe that is what saved my life. More about that in a while!

Denise's Story of Isolation: A unique event Denise's father used was "movie and popcorn night" to isolate her from her friends and others in the family. He would schedule a time when just the two of them would watch a movie together. This night was unique, indeed. You see, Denise's father laced her special popcorn with Oxy.IR, a form of the drug

Oxycodone, which is a potent opioid drug. When taken, it changes how your body feels and responds to pain.

Unknowingly, Denise consumed this drugged popcorn, which rendered her numb and incoherent. As a result, Denise has foggy memories and a strong sense of denial.

This confusion also caused her to feel a sense of dependency on her father's care and special treatment. He tricked her into believing this movie and popcorn time was just for her. In retrospect, this "unique event" was her father's way of keeping her from going out with her friends.

Threats: Abusers commonly use threats to assure you will keep the abuse a secret. Your abuser may have threatened to hurt or kill you, your siblings, other family members, or even pets. They may also have threatened to commit suicide, get fired, or go to jail.

Jane's Story of Threats: When I was in junior and senior high school, Mr. Petersen molested me; he was a math teacher, basketball coach, and trusted faculty member. Though he was married and had two young children, he drew me in with his charm and comforting support. He used his skills to manipulate me for over a year and a half into believing I was in love with him. Get this: I used to say to friends, "I have a boyfriend, but I can't tell you who."

What I defined as a relationship was a fantasy. Talk about programming! Mr. Petersen used to tell me that our relationship and love could not be public, or he would get fired. He would inform me he was at risk of going to jail and being banned from ever teaching again. Also, he confessed if anyone knew about our relationship, he would have to commit suicide to survive the exposure of our love. OH BOY! He was a master!

Denise's Story of Threats: Denise was the family peacekeeper. She was sure that if she didn't cooperate, all hell would break loose with her mother. Her father told Denise that he was obligated to be in alliance with his wife. His continued abandonment threats put Denise in a state of perpetual fear of losing her relationship with him. Her only desire was to be loved and special. When she was used as a pawn between her parents, the threat of losing their love was devastating.

Intimidation: While intimidation is very similar to the abuser threatening you in various ways, I believe the difference is slight and unrecognizable. In my interpretation, a threat is obvious and can be extreme. On the other hand, your abuser will use intimidation as a subtle strategy designed to scare you into submission. Such tactics might have included threatening looks or gestures, or maybe your abuser "accidentally" smashed things in front of you, destroyed property, hurt your pets, or put weapons on display. The subtle message was that if you didn't obey now, there would be violent consequences later.

Jane's Story of Intimidation: To illustrate the difference between a threat and intimidation, I can describe the contrast of how two of my family members acted.

One of my brothers in particular was extremely threatening, intimidating, and violent. He would use force to make me submit. As I stated before, I would be dragged down the hallway with my wrists in one of his giant hands. He would throw open the door and push me down, promptly taking charge. In my effort to prevent specific actions, I would lock my jaw closed. Unfortunately, that didn't stop his "creativity" and the decision to follow through with his actions.

Since I was about six years old when this began, he would use physical aggression and threatening words to render me powerless.

On the other hand, my father was very subtle and intimidating. He had a particular look, a tilt of his head, and silence that spoke volumes. As my memories were surfacing, I recall one specific occasion when I shared with him about my brother's abuse. He concurred saying it had absolutely one hundred percent happened. I asked him where he was while it was happening. He immediately jerked his head in my direction with the ever-familiar tilt and an intense stare that triggered immediate paralysis and panic in me. With his simple look and silence, I experienced a dangerous regression; he mastered submission.

Denise's Story of Intimidation: Denise viewed her father as bigger than life. She recalls a poem she wrote in high school, which won her enthusiastic support from her teachers. They expressed what an ideal father he was and how much he loved her, supporting her image of him.

As a child, she described her father as Job from the Bible, known for overcoming great tragedies to demonstrate his love for God. She grew up believing he could do no wrong.

However, she kept the secret because she was intimidated by the power of her father's presence and his kindness to others. Denise felt overwhelmed by her father's ability to roll with the punches and deal with many injuries and back surgeries. Even though she always felt less than deserving, she held her father in the highest esteem, dedicated to preserving his image at all costs.

Her intense need to protect her father's image continued into adulthood when she worked with him at his CPA firm. He had become severely addicted to alcohol and prescription pills. Denise was at his side, believing it was on her shoulders if she could not step in and maintain the family business.

As a result of this intimidation, Denise realized she was trusting those who appeared to be larger than life, like Job, experts in what they do and what they know. After being a victim of those taking advantage of women unaware of how to stand in their power, her healing shifted in the last two years when she understood the source of intimidation and the magnitude of inaccurate perceptions.

Denial and Blame: These classic tactics cause you to question your reality.

The blame game results in the abuser shifting the responsibility to you. I believe this is one of the most effective mind control tools used in our lives in both the past and the present. When there was denial, if you did speak up, your abuser lied, casting doubt on your story and sometimes causing you to doubt yourself.

Jane's Story of Denial and Blame: Throughout my life, my abusers blamed my abuse on my cousin, teachers, uncles, and brothers-in-law. I recall my father and brother joining forces one time to blame my cousin, Billy. They would tell stories of Billy dragging me down the hall to the bedroom with one hand around my wrists. Does this story sound familiar? Yes, to me as well, as this method was my brother's regular modus operandi.

Denise's Story of Denial and Blame: The most significant struggle for Denise and MOST others is self-doubt and seemingly endless denial. Abusers, including Denise's father, are crafty, brilliant, and overachievers at "gaslighting." Gaslighting is a tactic in which a person or entity can gain more power, making victims question their reality. It works much better than you may think.

Anyone is susceptible to gaslighting, and it is a common technique of abusers, dictators, narcissists, and cult leaders. It is done slowly so the victim doesn't realize how much they've been brainwashed. Ironically, Denise describes her family as the picture-perfect life. BINGO!

Gaslighting was working on behalf of her abuser, her father. Denise's brother describes their parents as the masters of mind manipulation. Convinced the family had no issues, the kids believed the family looked beautiful from the outside. Denise's denial is completely understandable due to being drugged and both parents' mind games.

Blame was a vicious cycle for her family. Denise's father would blame her mother, and her mother would turn it around to be Denise's fault. The process of blame is an emotional and mental jigsaw puzzle. And that is why we have to reveal the missing peace. (See what I did there?)

*   *   *

Here is a doozy of a story. Shortly after I began my quest to confront my family, I found out my brother and father went to see my therapist, Marjorie, behind my back. Marjorie was my personal therapist, not our family therapist. She believed my father and brother were coming to see how they could support me. When they arrived for their appointment, however, she found out their intentions were very different.

My brother and father began drilling Marjorie for information about me and reported that my cousin and individuals did the abuse outside of the home. My brother also began informing Marjorie of my *sexual identity crisis*. She did everything she could to maintain her safety and composure as she escorted them out the door. Here is the kicker: neither of them had been confronted by me about their abuse yet! Why in the world would they plead innocence without being designated as the abusers at that time? Guilty much?!

I want to spend more time on the topic of denial because it is the number one challenge that many survivors, including me, deal with in life. Please understand that even though I am not a psychologist, psychiatrist, Master of Social Work (MSW), Licensed Social Worker (LSW), nor am I a therapist, I do understand the power of the mind.

Our mind is a powerful tool and can provide us the necessary coping mechanism to survive any level of trauma. Some will refer to trauma survivors as having dissociative disorders. (I mentioned this earlier in this chapter about my father.) Dissociative disorders are an involuntary escape from reality characterized by a disconnection between thoughts, identity, consciousness, and memory.

People from all age groups and racial, ethnic, and socioeconomic backgrounds can experience a dissociative disorder. The National Alliance on Mental Illness reports that up to seventy-five percent of people experience at least one episode of feeling disconnected from themselves or their environment, while only two percent meet the full criteria for chronic episodes. Women are more likely than men to be diagnosed with a dissociative disorder.

Numerous therapists have told me about my dissociative disorder "style." This style of surviving apparently allowed me to endure the pain and reality of the actions perpetrated against me. Have you ever had an "out of body" experience while being abused, or a sense or feeling of being "beside yourself"? Well, you were; that was dissociative disorder at work. We have the ability to remove ourselves or numb out on all levels to survive.

Let me help you understand how that style may still apply to you today. Many years ago, I went to the doctor to get a mole on my neck removed–a simple procedure, but apparently, one that is considered very painful. Per the doctor, the shot alone for the procedure put men in tears, and that was before the removal process. When the doctor plunged the long needle into my neck, I didn't move, let alone flinch. He froze and asked me if I was still alive. I smiled and said I was ready for the remaining steps. I could tell by the look on his face that I was not his average patient.

I realized I had been numb most of my life, and this experience was no exception. Yes, I couldn't feel needles, but my numbness prevented me from feeling the good things, the hugs, pinches, smooches, and loving. Today, as a survivOR, trust me, I cannot even get a few acupuncture needles without tearing up and wiggling my way off the table in pain. This change is because I have thawed out.

One of my goals is to help you thaw out, too. Get ready to feel every hug, pinch, and smooch. Denise has been thawing out over the last handful of years. She always had a high pain tolerance, and she thought the reason was from experiencing two Cesarean section births. Now she realizes where it came from and can feel a lot more than she has in years.

You, too, may have excessive levels of pain tolerance or have put up with far too much chaos, drama, and abuse. I want you to know that this is because of your training and programming. You had to step outside of yourself to live through both the physical pain and the emotional devastation.

When I became aware of my dissociative style, I created a list of symptoms in response to my traumatic events. The dissociative style helped me keep my memories under control and suppressed. Under stressful situations, do you find the feeling of being "beside yourself" increases symptoms and creates problems with functioning in everyday activities?

First, let me say I realize everyone can relate to being "beside yourself," whether or not they have experienced abuse. My goal is to move you from numbing out to your feelings to the OR style of living. We will shake it up now, move on, and reach a place where we never have to look back at what is wrong or broken.

Signs and Symptoms

Another goal I have is to teach you to recognize the signs or symptoms *before* you experience a profound emotional reaction to your past. Instead, the idea is for you to have a neutral curiosity in response to these signs or symptoms. The following is a list of ways that symptoms of abuse can show up:

- Feeling you are innately flawed
- Believing that no one understands you
- Feeling self-hatred
- Experiencing hopelessness
- Carrying the burden of feeling powerless
- Feeling like an imposter (Imposter Syndrome): thinking if people found out who you are, they would not stay
- Feeling blue, depressed, lacking motivation
- Experiencing anger
- Having an addiction to porn, sex, or toys
- Controlling and together on the outside, yet holding the secret inside
- Implementing self-sabotaging behaviors
- Lacking trust
- Sensing or feeling fear
- Having no follow-through
- Suffering from an inner sense of being so far behind everyone else due to your past
- Shutting down or becoming numb and unable to express feelings
- Acting in a co-dependent way
- Lacking limits or boundaries
- Suffering from addiction or addictive behavior: food, chemicals, sex, chaos, drama, sex, self-sabotage, abuse
- Sensing there are blamers and playing victim to the world
- Experiencing panic attacks, anxiety, and being overly stressed
- Suffering from nightmares, insomnia, or sleep disruption
- Lacking commitment
- Having affairs and being unfaithful or desiring to act on inner needs

- Succumbing to abusive relationships
- Not being great receivers or givers
- Bearing the stress of body dysmorphia, embarrassment, or shame
- Being needy, clingy, desperate, and exhausting
- Testing of others to determine safety
- Lacking self-esteem, confidence, and worthiness
- Feeling undeserving of love, affection, and commitment
- Leaving before you should have left or staying way too long in a relationship
- Experiencing sexual fantasies linked to feelings of shame, guilt, humiliation, and being dirty
- Ensuring sexual encounters are planned, controlled, predictable, and expected
- Spending most of the time in your head during intimacy
- Being unforgiving and bitter

Now that we've identified the list of signs and symptoms, we will begin checking off the numerous effects of abuse and move into a more incredible version of you. You will drive the wheel of power and control. We will dig up all the emotions, memories, and triggers to release them for your fully evolved *OR* life. Instead of being triggered by these signs or symptoms, you can be mindful of them and mildly curious. In this way, you regain control. So, let's start with memories.

Triggers

Anything that reminds you of your past is a trigger, good or bad, bringing back memories related to your life events, not only the abuse. For example, you know *that song*. *That song* that makes you remember your high school prom or first kiss. Maybe it is *that song* that reminds you of springtime and the best vacation you ever had growing up. Or *that song* reminded you of the first time he or she touched you. Music, or a person, smell, feeling, touch, taste, or view can instantly bring back memories.

While triggers themselves are usually harmless, they cause your body to react as if you're in danger. You may feel like you're living through it all over again. I am a firm believer in knowing your triggers, neutralizing them, and navigating life without requiring clear memories. I do NOT believe anyone needs to have a movie reel of their abuse in order to heal. You need to accept and acknowledge that you have experienced violation, touch or no touch.

CHAPTER 2

Uncover the Memories

Memories

Memories are how we retain information to influence future action. Memory is the brain's faculty that encodes, stores, and retrieves data or information when needed; memories are the product of our minds. If not for remembering past events, it would be impossible for language, relationships, or personal identity to develop.

Great, so memories are facts that help us establish that an event or experience occurred. This process should be simple. However, it often isn't.

You begin questioning your life as you grow up and get a sense something has occurred:

Fact: I feel like I experienced abuse.

Fact: It seems to have begun at birth and continued until I was fifteen years old.

Fact: I have all the signs of a sexual abuse survivor.

Fact: I don't trust many members of my family.

Fact: I feel I regress when I am around specific individuals.

After making these statements to ourselves, we may state what feels like a fact, and even go as far as to share it with others. But when we attempt to share the details, we may get nothing! We may find no data, no recall, no reviving facts, events, or impressions. NOTHING!

Therefore, not having seen any data, our logical mind says FALSE. As a result, we begin to deny our sense of truth and require memories to prove our case. If this happens to us, we may have memory suppression.

In my case, I had suppressed my abuse memories until I began therapy at the age of twenty-five. Fortunately, or unfortunately (I am still not sure yet), my memories came flooding back to me within the first year of investigation.

I question the gift of my memories. First and foremost, it is fortunate I could remember what happened, or else I may not have believed it was true. On the other hand, I would often prefer not to have the "movies" that run in my mind reflecting my abuse.

Denise's lack of memories, on the other hand, plagues her for a different reason. A few years ago, she began having dreams that confused her. She saw flashes from her early life that did not match what she recalled about her childhood. As time progressed these dreams and flashes expanded, so she began doing research. She had suspicions around sexual abuse but never attributed them to her family. While my memories were vivid and detailed, hers were not. They continue to be foggy visions and feelings of intense familiarity in certain situations, causing her doubt. She has doubted herself, been overly trusting with most people, and has backed down more often than she has stood in her power.

Since she does not have "movie" memories, Denise has an inner struggle of doubt and assurance, two sides of the same coin. She knows something happened to her; she is sure. However, in her attempts to access details or clear pictures, Denise continues to feel familiarity and see only blurred memories of the incidents. For example, she discovered while journaling that there is a part of her not willing to remember. Her hand would not write the words I want to remember in her journal. She could write should and need, but not want.

When I share my story of abuse with Denise, she can relate to my experience and feels the same way; the only difference is I have the movies and details. She has no movie-type memories, but she has feelings and related physical reactions.

Either way, whether you have "movie" memories like me, or if you identify impressions and feelings with no concrete "data" like Denise, please know that memories are NOT proof of truth. Truth makes up your feelings and reactions, which provide you with enough evidence to heal, powerfully.

Our memories serve us in many ways. However, what happens when our memories are nonexistent, or foggy at best? Denise is not alone in this regard. When they do not remember or know all of the details, most people slip into doubt and reject the idea of abuse. Lack of substantial evidence can both delay your healing process and leave you open to ridicule. The topic of abuse is not one to be taken lightly. It isn't an opinion you state to others and waver in your stance.

For example, when I was beginning to remember my abuse, I had an incredible amount of memories flooding my mind. Why? I demanded that my memory system function. Be careful what you wish for, though! I knew if I were the only person in my family to confront the generations of abuse, I would need to stand strong. For me, standing strong meant I had to have firm evidence with as many details as possible. NOT everyone needs all the details. Truth be told, as I look back, I realized I didn't have every detail, but I was convinced no one would believe me if I didn't have a solid case.

Guess what? No one believed me anyway! All the recall and work I did to gather evidence only served to provide me a false sense of strength. Some family members called me crazy and accused me of having a sexual identity problem. They told everyone I had no other way to hide behind my issue, except to blame them for abuse.

I know some of you will have a hard time with this idea about not requiring "movie" memories. You may insist that if you don't have memories, no one will believe you (including you). I want to ask you: do you prefer to cling to this belief, or are you ready to move on and become a survivOR? I urge you to move forward whether you have specific "movie memories" or not if you have a gut feeling about experiencing abuse.

Your mind is vital to your process of becoming a survivOR. Your readiness will reveal your past. It is not a practice of demanding that the flood gates open and there your memories are for you to embrace. Denise's therapist shared with her the story of a man who demanded to break through the memory barrier. He went through a controversial treatment designed to crack open the vault of memories which left this man significantly damaged.

Do not seek to crack the vault open all at once. One of my main goals for sharing Revealing the Missing Peace is to let you know that you do not have to relive the abuse or trauma to heal. If you begin to see a bit of denial breaking down and a slice of memory attempting to surface, be patient. We will be walking through the memory process in the coming chapters. Hang tight!

Calling Up Memories

Let's look at how to reveal the hidden memories in our subconscious mind. Remember, according to Northwestern's study, the way to do this is to relive your past. I am going to suggest we bypass the past and avoid reliving the trauma. We will look at the workings of the mind in the coming chapters that will demonstrate why living trauma over and over again begets more trauma patterns in the brain. And there I go; I have already said too much. I tend to get ahead of myself!

The process of unlocking memories frees us from addiction to patterns and behaviors, known as triggers. In Chapter 1, we also identified signs and symptoms.

Be cautious about cracking the vault when you do not have any memories. The next steps offer a different approach, a gentle, loving way to massage the mind and bring forth memories. This method is the most significant work you are going to do. If you do not have memories, please walk through the following steps to patiently reveal your past.

Step 1: Memory Work Begins with Permission.

Trauma causes us to repress or store memories to keep us safe and functioning. As you begin investigating your memory bank and seeking evidence of abuse or any experience, you must be open. You must allow yourself the freedom to remember.

I made a conscious decision to remember. I asked my subconscious mind to reveal some of the abuse in my childhood. Every day, I set aside time to journal, draw, meditate, script, or listen to music to open my mind to receive the relevant memories. Keep in mind you do not need specific, concrete, "movie" memories to validate your healing. You simply need to know in your heart your abuse happened.

Step 2: Safety First!

You must set up a safe environment to open to the past. I did my memory work in several ways.

    a. **Traditional therapy** is one option as you go through your healing. However, I spent many years and many hours going over my story, often drenched in a full-on sweat when I walked out of the therapy office. I firmly believe we need to stop telling the story. I will show you evidence of a new way to reveal the missing peace. My mission is to make this work easy; breaking out in a sweat is unnecessary.

b. **Emotion-Focused Therapy (EFT)** is a therapeutic approach based on the premise that emotions are central to our identity and provide valuable information. According to EFT, emotions guide our choices and decisions; lacking emotional awareness or avoiding unpleasant emotions can harm us.

c. **Eye Movement Desensitization and Reprocessing (EMDR)** is a psychotherapy treatment initially designed to alleviate the distress associated with traumatic memories (Shapiro, 1989a, 1989b). [1] EMDR was one of my all-time favorite methods of therapy work in my healing. EMDR therapy helped me unearth traumatic emotions related to my memories and release their power over me. It was a process in which my therapist utilized rapid eye movement and sound stimulation to generate repressed memories. I found it to be a fast, easy method to remember and move through the resulting feelings and reactions. I am all about shortcutting any process, and EMDR was a great way to make that happen.

d. **PSYCH-K ® (Psychological Kinesiology)** is designed to help people change the way they feel, behave, and interact in life. PSYCH-K ® focuses on changing subconscious beliefs. The idea is that by changing behavior, feelings, and interpretations in recurring situations in life, individuals can modify their state of mind at the first indication of stress.

e. **Drawing** was my primary method of journaling and one of the helpful healing tools in my work. I spent hours drawing my feelings, and many times they would develop organically into memories. It was as if I would go into a hypnotic state, and my hand would begin sketching my life right before my eyes. I would get lost in the drawings, and the feelings would pour onto the pages through the images.

f. **Scripting** involves writing out a conversation between you and your younger or abused self, useful for extracting memories and feelings. Scripting is like writing a script for a play. You begin with your initial and message, then answer with your younger self's initial and response. Here is an example of an exchange:

> J: I would love to know what might have happened between my father and me.
>
> LJ: (Little Jane): Nothing.
>
> J: If something did happen, what might it be?
>
> LJ: I do remember one time–or more.

g. **Journaling:** Good old-fashioned journaling or free writing is a healing tool that allows you to "data dump" all of the stories, emotions, and thoughts running through you.

---

[1] https://www.emdr.com/what-is-emdr/

This beneficial communication method helps you to express yourself without even making sense of it or being able to read it. The process is simply a step in dumping the old and creating the new.

h. **Art Therapy** involves using creative techniques such as drawing, painting, collage, coloring, or sculpting to help people express themselves and examine the psychological and emotional undertones in their art. I worked in the drug and alcohol treatment center with several art therapists. I learned from them and became skillful at "decoding" the nonverbal messages, symbols, and metaphors often found in these art forms. We worked together with the patients to better understand their feelings and behaviors as they unraveled deeper issues and root causes of their addiction. We are all addicted to our feelings, so I will walk you through our feeling addictions in the coming chapters. Stay tuned–it will be quite an eye-opener for you.

i. **Hypnotherapy:** Never in a million years did I believe hypnosis would work on me. I never wanted to let go of control. In my endless search for help, however, I decided to give it a try.

As you may know, guided hypnosis is a trance-like state of focus and concentration which is similar to being completely absorbed in a book, movie, music, daydreaming, or meditation. In this state, you can turn your attention completely inward to find and utilize the natural resources deep within. These resources can help you make changes or regain control in specific areas of your life.

j. **Family Role Play Therapy** played a significant role in dislodging memories for me. Actually, a role-play session first introduced to me the possibility that I had experienced abuse. This realization was a powerful jolt to my system. Let me set the scene (see what I did there, role play-scene). My first role-play encounter was at a workshop with my primary therapist. Each person in the group was selected to play one of my family members. Did I mention I am the youngest of seven kids and have a huge extended family? We had a full stage with me as the audience member. I gave them the back story of how my family would gather for holidays and described the interaction. AND ACTION!

The role-playing began and I believe I went into shock. The suggestive interaction triggered my memory vault, and it began to take off like Old Faithful. As a geyser of memories started to flood my mind's eye, I was shocked and relieved all at the same time. Keep in mind, if you want to try this, you must do this therapy with a trained professional. It is powerful, and there is a risk of too much too fast. As you get to know me, you will find I have been a too-fast and too-much person my entire life. My most remarkable healing is to slow down. Do you drive yourself as I do? If so, being able to pace yourself is your most impactful work in the world.

k. **Regression Therapy** dedicates focus to uncovering things from your past that may be contributing to your current mental state, harmful habits, or addictions. There are two types of regression therapy: age regression therapy and past-life regression therapy. The design of the first type targets your past, so I chose it because I wanted to uncover what happened during my childhood. I didn't experience the second type focusing on past lives as I was more concerned with getting today's life straightened out.

l. **Neuro-Linguistic Programming (NLP)** is a psychological approach that analyzes strategies used by successful individuals and then applies them to reach a personal goal. It relates thoughts, language, and patterns of behavior learned through experience to specific outcomes. I have been using this method more recently in my ongoing evolution. It is fast, and the shifts in my thinking are quick.

m. *GO Therapy* is my invention. I am a physical and verbal processor. I need movement and physical activity to release emotions effectively; otherwise, I become tired, cranky, angry, and my muscles stiffen up. That state resulted in stagnant thinking and creativity. It is vital to MOVE! Since our muscles hold emotions, I believe it is necessary to install new information to them through movement.

n. **Reiki** is a very specific form of energy healing, in which hands are placed just off the body or lightly touching the body, as in "laying on of hands." The intention is to create deep relaxation, to help speed healing, reduce pain, and decrease other symptoms you may be experiencing. I found this form of therapy extremely helpful for sorting out my memories and feelings. Reiki worked on many levels of my life, spiritually, physically, emotionally, and mentally. Also, it was so relaxing and nurturing.

o. **Inner Child Work** was a HUGE part of my process, past and present. Internal Family Systems (IFS) is an approach to psychotherapy that identifies and addresses multiple sub-personalities or families within each person's mental system. These sub-personalities consist of wounded parts (painful emotions such as anger and shame), and other parts that try to control and protect the person from their pain.

The sub-personalities are often in conflict with each other and with one's Core Self, a concept that describes the confident, compassionate, whole person at every individual's core. IFS focuses on healing the wounded parts and restoring mental balance and harmony by changing the dynamics that create discord among the sub-personalities and the self.

Step 3: Pick a Winner!

There are numerous forms of therapy, almost too many to name. Select a method to begin working on unlocking or further revealing memories and feelings from your past, affecting your present and future.

Inner System

My winner by a mile for therapy in a safe environment is the inner child work. I have dedicated my healing to understanding my inner children and the role each plays in my life. I am sure I'm dating myself. You may have heard of the 1976 movie with Sally Field called Sybil, a true story about a young woman with sixteen personalities.

It's interesting to note that American transpersonal philosopher Ken Wilber and English humanistic psychologist John Rowan suggested that the average person has about a dozen sub-personalities.

I will warn you that you will likely feel like Sybil as you go through this work. I will walk you through some of my processes working with the inner child, or children, more accurately.

During my abuse, I found my system was able to create support personality traits or what I call my inner child. I discovered my personality traits are a semi-independent sub-personality subordinate to the waking conscious mind. A sub-personality is a personality mode that temporarily activates to allow a person to cope with certain psychosocial situations.

Sub-personalities or inner child traits allowed us to make it through the trauma we endured. I was able to survive each day of my childhood by utilizing this coping skill. A great way to think of this is to compare it to our fight-or-flight response. When we encounter a stressful situation, we naturally respond without consciously deciding on it. It evolved as a survival mechanism, enabling us to react quickly to life-threatening conditions. The carefully orchestrated yet near-instantaneous sequence of hormonal changes and physiological responses help us fight the threat or flee to safety. I compare this same survival response to the development of our inner child/children. I have yet to meet anyone who has just one inner child. For the purpose of this work, let's assume I am referring to many inner personality traits or children.

These traits or inner children have served us well. Each trait allowed us to navigate our childhood and adult life. Unfortunately, our system tends to overreact to stressors or triggers that are not life-threatening, such as traffic jams, work pressure, and family difficulties. The stressor feels familiar, and our training through our inner personalities or sub-personalities causes us to react instantaneously. Even though we are no longer in a life-threatening situation, our inner child doesn't understand the difference.

Let me give you a great example of my inner system taking over and overreacting. In high school, my sister and her friends thought it would be fun to go through a haunted house. First, let me share with you–anyone who has grown up in fear has NO business going into a haunted house. Nevertheless, I allowed them to convince me to join them, thinking how fun it would be.

I am sure you know exactly where this story is going. We skillfully navigated the sharp turns and dark corridors surrounded by echoing sounds of screams and horror-filled sound effects. We made it safely through the house until the last turn of the tour. A breeze began to blow from a skillfully hidden fan. The sounds dimmed, and we all let out a sigh of relief. We made it. NO! We didn't! As we passed a curtain, out jumped one of the haunted house workers dressed as a giant zombie. Everyone screamed. I proceeded to ball up my fist in an instant and deliver a blow to the zombie's gut!

My reaction was immediate and overreactive. My inner child believed I was in imminent danger and triggered my response. I felt awful about myself. I am sure I knocked the wind out of the poor guy dressed as a zombie merely doing his job.

Inner Child Work Begins with Awareness. Because our past programs us, there have been many knee-jerk reactions, overreacting to situations. By adapting to actions, conditions, messages, abuse, and other environmental input, we developed a coping mechanism to survive whenever we encounter any stimuli.

Understanding this is key to healing and revealing the missing peace. We need self-awareness and an awareness of others and their effect on us. I believe the fact that you are reading this book shows me you are either awake or waking up. You don't need to know all of your triggers or the why and where of them. You must be aware there are situations, people, and environments that will elicit a negative or old response in you.

Let me share another example of a knee-jerk reaction and how I learned to identify it. My family had an advanced ability to tease to the point of abuse. We were programmed to turn on each other. There was no support structure or safety in numbers as it was everyone for themselves. Your goal was to get to the top of the hill, hope no one pushed you off, and take out your opponents.

In my adult life, I discovered I was overly sensitive to teasing, even for something small. I would shut down and go into my programmed belief I was not enough or something was epically wrong with me. It would throw me so far off into the weeds that I could barely think clearly. I would turn red and be on the verge of tears.

My inner child was programmed to believe it was my fault. When I found myself in these situations, there was no rational thought to turn it around. When I was triggered and operating from my inner child, I could not see the teasing as a way for the person to get to know me or a sign of comfort and connection. To me, all teasing was threatening and delivered for the sole purpose of making me less than adequate or worthy. Knowing that I felt this way about teasing allowed me to become mindful of it and address it.

Awareness is vital in putting Humpty Dumpty back together again. I believe to survive we fragment to save ourselves. We have warriors or protectors that develop in our inner children to withstand the variety of situations we encounter. We designed them to protect ourselves and ensure our survival. Without these parts of ourselves, we may not be here today.

VITAL INFORMATION: When referencing our inner child/children, we MUST know they are only a PART of us. They are not the whole of who we are. Therefore, we must take on the role of guardian.

How do you know if an inner child is running you? First, identify behaviors you demonstrate as a result of your environment. We all have destructive behaviors we act out in various forms. These vary from subtle self-sabotage and self-defeating patterns to passive hostility to severe self-destructive symptoms, violent aggression, and, sometimes, criminal behavior. Commonly, destructive behavior in adults bears the impulsive quality of childish temper tantrums. Or inner children can show up as neediness, dependency, and dread of abandonment.

Common Behaviors

I have created a list of behaviors commonly displayed by survivors of sexual abuse, touch or non-touch:

- High levels of depression
- Guilt
- Shame

- Self-blame
- Eating disorders
- Somatic concerns
- Anxiety
- Dissociative patterns
- Repression
- Denial
- Sexual problems
- Relationship problems
- Self-mutilation/cutting/injuries
- Domestic violence
- Addictions to chemicals, sex, porn, food, people, etc.
- Suicidal tendencies
- Phobias
- Self judgement
- Abuse of others or self
- Neglect of self

The long-term effects of the abuse that the survivor experiences, such as depression and dissociative patterns, affect the survivor's sexual functioning.

In the next book in this series, Revealing the Edge, we will look more in-depth at sexual symptoms that often result from experiences of sexual abuse. These will include the following and are not limited to:

- Avoidance
- Fear
- Lack of interest
- Approaching sex as an obligation
- Experiencing negative feelings such as anger, disgust, or guilt with touch
- Having difficulty becoming aroused or feeling any sensation
- Feeling emotionally distant or not present during sex
- Experiencing intrusive or disturbing sexual thoughts and images

- Engaging in compulsive or inappropriate sexual behaviors
- Experiencing difficulty establishing or maintaining an intimate relationship
- Experiencing vaginal pain or orgasmic problems (women); and experiencing erectile, ejaculatory, or orgasmic difficulties (men and women)

The bottom line is that any degree of abuse, touch or non-touch, will leave a lasting program or pattern of behavior, and it is our job to be aware of our actions.

Creating and Using Your List

Start a list of behaviors or thoughts that you demonstrate regularly. You may also want to make a list based on particular situations.

For example, while growing up, I was told I was fat, dumb, and stupid. Over and over again my sister, father, and brother reinforced my belief I was dumb. Sexual abuse instills deep-seated programming in which we believe something is wrong, and for me, it reinforced the dummy button programmed in my belief system. No matter what I did in life, I was the dumb kid, and I proved it by being the first to sit down in the spelling bee. I was an average student and doubted myself every step of the way.

I worked on becoming aware of the trigger; I am fat, dumb, and stupid. Early on in therapy sessions, I was sure I had defeated this belief until the age of forty when I became an entrepreneur. If you want to stir up your emotional issues, start your own business. My dummy button was alive and kicking the minute I tried to grow my business and sell myself to my clients. I felt utterly unworthy and doubted the fact I was smart enough to be a businesswoman. As a result, I began to avoid sales calls and delayed doing the money-making tasks that would prove I was qualified to be in that position, based on my past. My response was self-abuse. My self-talk was devastating. I would never say to others what I was continually saying to myself. I judged, humiliated, guilted, and shamed myself, reinforcing my belief I am fat, dumb, and stupid, and will never be enough.

Examples that illustrate situational behavior include sexual encounters. In college, I found myself getting involved with older men, many of whom were married. My training was to believe relationships were a replication of my abuse by my father. I was seeking encounters that reinforced my role at home. As a result, my meetings with men were secretive, seductive, episodic, dirty, covert, devious, sly, and stealthy. Sexual encounters were overwhelmingly triggering situations that continued to anchor in my feelings of guilt, shame, blame, worthiness, and overall brokenness.

The greater awareness you have of your behaviors, beliefs, and actions, the greater your chance of living in true PEACE. Please make a list, check it twice, and add anything you missed the first time.

The next step and the best way to identify with your inner self and connect with the inner child/children is to use your list. I want to share with you my method of inner relationship building.

1. **Dig out any childhood pictures of yourself.** If you don't have any, search online or in magazines to find what you imagine you looked like as a kid. All ages are going to show up for you, so gather as many as you would like.

2. **Select the first image that jumps out at you.** Give this little one a name. For example, I had a little three-year-old who jumped out as my first inner part asking for healing. I named her Savannah.

3. **Write a letter to the adult you are now from this little one.** If you are at a loss for words, write a question with your dominant hand. You may ask a simple question like: Why are you here with me today? Now with your non-dominant hand, write the answer. You will be surprised what will pour out of you.

4. **Read and sit with the letter for a few days.** Be patient, accepting, and never judge what is in the message.

5. **Search for a stuffed animal, statue, or symbol that represents this little one.**

6. **Each day, spend time communicating, cuddling, or sitting with this part of you.** Allow further information to be revealed.

7. **Begin to identify the feelings and behaviors associated with this part.** It is essential you clearly understand the role this part of you plays in your life. Let's say this little one is the gatekeeper and does not trust anyone. If this little one is allowed to run free, you will face challenges in relationships, trust, follow-through, friendships, and find yourself lonely or alone. You must know the role this little one plays.

8. **Now ask your adult self: Does this role serve my current life? Or: Was this role key in my childhood, and is it no longer necessary?**

9. **Determine if this part of you is vital in your present world.** If so, carry on. If not, you have a decision to make. You can either give this part a new role or send it on its way. I have retired some parts of me. I do this by allowing my mother's spirit to take them with her to the world beyond the physical. With others, I have given them new jobs. I found that my protector, JW, is the best vetting employee I have in my business. This part of me can say who will be a good fit or a drain in my business.

10. **EVERY PART of you played an influential, significant role in your life.** Honor each part of you and express gratitude for them, helping you survive.

11. Create a future for this part of you through visualization or any other method of visioning.

The process of listing your behaviors and thoughts, and then connecting to your Inner child/children through this list, will help you put Humpty Dumpty back together again. This work is instrumental in staying in your adult and higher self as you navigate a world that can feel like a minefield at times. We need to put ourselves together as one cohesive, empowered person.

The work you do with your inner child(ren) is ongoing. We continue to encounter triggering situations that stir up our system of predictable old behaviors. If we are not fully aware and communicating with ourselves, our younger selves will run the show. Discovering the new and improved parts of you is vital to embracing and liberating them. Practice awareness daily and design a path for inner peace! Here are some quotes to get you started:

"If you are depressed, you are living in the past. If you are anxious, you are living in the future. If you are at peace, you are living in the present."

—Lao Tzu

"Do not let the behavior of others destroy your inner peace."

—The Dalai Lama

"Peace can become a lens through which you see the world. Be it. Live it. Radiate it out. Peace is an inside job."

—Wayne Dyer

"Outward peace is useless without inner peace."

—Mahatma Gandhi

My goal for you, reading this book, is to guide you through the process to reveal inner peace and radiate true PEACE.

CHAPTER 3

Reveal the Truth

*L*ike the crash of cymbals coming together on a warm spring day during my senior year of college, my fist exploded through my dorm room window. I lived on the third story of the upper-class dorms, and my partner had beaten me for the last time; I felt trapped, alone, and crazy. No one understood me, nor did I know myself. As I stood with blood dripping down my hand and glass shattering on the sidewalk below, I dropped to my knees and pleaded for help.

I was twenty-two years old and felt like something was wrong with me. Random fights and physical abuse in my volatile relationship riddled my life; this treatment was familiar to me. Yet, on this day, I was done. I decided I would do whatever it took to find the right help to allow me to feel *normal*.

I took it upon myself to secretly find a therapist who would tell me what was wrong, what was going on with me, and how to fix it. Wow, that would have been great!

I didn't realize therapy was a process of talking until you figure out what is wrong.

Okay, I exaggerate, although I did walk through the door to my therapist, expecting to be fixed and left feeling just as messed up. Yes, I was a senior in college and desperate for the answer. What I didn't realize at that time is the issue was my abuse. I had no memories or even a hint of any level of abuse. Get this; I believed I had a great family except for my mom's alcoholism. By the time I completed my memory work, however, there was no question why my mother drank.

Unfortunately, my mother didn't find her way free from the abusers. She drank herself to death when I was fourteen years old. I used to think that she was my problem. I discovered later that while she significantly contributed to the situation, she was the by-product.

For the next few years, I went from therapist to therapist, begging for answers. Some wanted to medicate me while others continued to focus on my mother's death. During my sessions, I shared about my sexual activities with older, married men, infidelities, fear of men, as well as a number of my classic symptoms common to survivors of sexual abuse:

- Self-harm and self-mutilation
- Continuous feelings of guilt, shame, and self-blame
- Feelings of worthlessness, doubt, fear, and low self-esteem
- Endless nightmares and visions of people standing over my bed
- Erratic behavior, such as aggression, anger, hostility, or hyperactivity
- Depression, anxiety or unusual fears, or a sudden loss of self-confidence
- Rebellious or defiant behavior
- Body issues, such as seeing myself as fat, hating my breasts, being ashamed of my female genitalia, and more
- Somatization symptoms–mind/body connection–related to pelvic pain, gastrointestinal problems, and headaches
- Difficulties with trust, fear of intimacy, fear of being different or weird, difficulty establishing interpersonal boundaries, passive behaviors, and getting involved in abusive relationships (Surprise! I was!)

I was a classic poster child for someone who has experienced sexual abuse. I had no idea, and frankly, it was not the therapists' job to tell me my past. I would not have believed them if they did suggest abuse was an option, but I was dedicated to finding out why I felt so *off* and *broken*.

You see, the most challenging part of having memories and telling one's story is the reaction from friends, family, abusers, and the world. The thing that makes remembering and telling so challenging is we are, more than likely, doubting, questioning, judging, and denying the truth to ourselves. I know now that there was a part of me who truly knew about the abuse and another part of me keeping me safe.

*   *   *

Disclaimer:

In this chapter, I share an unfiltered glimpse of my memories, to help you stand firm while you give way to your past and permit yourself to tell your story and truth, keeping yourself safe in the process.

*   *   *

I have been gifted–or not–with a powerful memory. As I mentioned earlier, I demanded to retrieve all memories to assure I would not doubt while moving through my healing. For you to move forward through the chapter, my job is to keep you safe, so I decided to provide a few *Rules of the Road* for you to follow:

1. Do not think for a second you need to have this level of memory recall to reveal the missing peace.
2. Do not compare your abuse to mine, or anyone else.
3. Do not condemn yourself for not remembering.
4. Do not force yourself to remember.
5. Do not minimize your experience.
6. Do not doubt, judge, shame, blame, or re-abuse yourself.
7. Do not run out and tell the world.

My Story

The day my life began, I was born the youngest of seven in the Chicagoland area. My father was a successful businessman providing for his family. Moving up the corporate ladder as the top sales professional for his company, my father's role in the engineering world required him to travel, entertain customers, and attend late-night meetings and countless company events. He was well-known with a prominent place in the community, and my parents engaged with many friends and social groups throughout the years. On the outside, we looked great! We had the house, the cars, status, income, achievements, and a great family portrait.

Unfortunately, behind closed doors, I lived an ongoing life of terror. Many little girls' bedtime routines included kissing and hugging their mom and dad goodnight, perhaps singing a lullaby, or snuggling up with a favorite storybook, but that was not the case for me.

My bedtime included laying in anticipation for the beginning of the nightly routine. With the flip of a switch, the hallway light streamed into my room and onto my bed. As I looked toward the doorway, the ever-familiar silhouette made its appearance. I learned early on there was no escaping the fate of what was about to happen next—and this continued for the following fourteen years.

I grew accustomed to what happened each night, but I was destined never to understand the all-too-familiar silence that filled the nightly air, a silence heavy with expectation and fear. Each day, I lived in fear of the darkness, of the ritual, a selection that always ended in pain. There was no sense in fighting, hoping, or praying for something different. I knew how the family system worked, a never-ending routine, a pattern, an existence that engulfed me in confusion, terror, shame, and a longing to escape.

My abuse goes back as far as I can remember. My earliest memory is being put in the crib for my nap and waking up needing a diaper change. My father came in and lifted me from the crib to change me. I recall being laid on a bed and him taking advantage of the quiet isolation of the room. Additional memories include my father calling me into the bathroom, bedroom, shower, basement, and garage. The most recent memory I have was my freshman year of high school.

I endured many days and nights of abuse by numerous members of my immediate family and extended family, as well as a few teachers. My father was the main perpetrator. And he ruled the family.

My mother, MaDonna, met my father when she was eighteen years old. Her father had lost the family farm due to alcoholism, and she dropped out of school to help support the family. My mother was being raised on welfare and had little to no self-esteem.

Born the youngest of twelve siblings, MaDonna Jean Fisher entered an abusive family plagued with alcoholism, bullying, and sexual abuse. My mother shared that she had several offenders in her family. Her brother tried drowning her in the bathtub; she was often pinned down by another, forcing her to submit to his power.

The family abuse left its impact on my mother's generation and beyond. A victim of her upbringing, she recreated the same life in adulthood. Three of her sisters were arrested repeatedly for prostitution. The police locked up two of her brothers for assault and theft.

My father, Ron, was born into a middle-class family, the first of three in his mother's second family. My grandmother had two children with her first husband before his tragic death in a freak accident while transporting a locomotive. A teenage boy was shooting at the train's bell, missed it, and shot my grandfather in the head.

My father, Ron, worked his way through engineering school and met my mother during his senior year. Ron shared with me that during his childhood, his father sexually abused him and his siblings. He had no memory of it until he pursued therapy after our confrontation meeting. (Yes, I confronted my father, which resulted in a significant boost to my healing. Stay tuned for the confrontation process.)

Learning My Truth

My truth was not so much revealed to me as I birthed it. I say birthed because it seems to be the one act that is extremely painful to endure. I fought to deny and suppress my memories every step of the way. I could not accept the fact of my abuse, and I was going to force those memories back down where they came from if it was my last thing I did. Unfortunately, I didn't have a choice in the matter. For as long as I can remember, I have been committed to making a difference in the world. This book, with my work through the pain, is the gift I am bringing forth.

My memories began in the form of nightmares. I would awaken almost every night in a full-blown panic, sweating through my pajamas, and reeling from the visions revealed. When I was growing up, I was deathly afraid of cats. Surprisingly, my visions came in the form of a cat's severed head in my pocket. This vicious cat's head was biting through my clothes into my genitals. I would quickly journal the nightmares and be ready to process them in my next therapy session.

The nightmares were easy to refute. I would rationalize the vision and relate it to my fear of cats. However, they progressed from a cat's head to real-life situations. I would wake to hear my siblings saying, "Hurry and let them go, Mom is coming!"

I would also have recurring nightmares about a gorilla running loose in the neighborhood and a giant candle in the house. Random? Yes. Telling? Definitely. My brother had what we referred to as a *sex candle* in his room. It was a giant candle with dripping wax running down the sides. This candle represented that a sexual encounter was inevitable or had already occurred. I had not remembered the candle until this dream. The gorilla represented the primitive behaviors of my perpetrators. Wild, unyielding, aggressive, and brutal actions had taken place over and over again.

My repeated nightmares of the severed cat's head was my system's way of slowly breaking the news to me about my abuse and the consequences. The sketch depicts the path of my memories unfolding. I was horrified and sympathetic of the cat at the same time. This shows how devastating it was to experience the horror of my memories.

Learning Your Truth

Your memories will come to you in many forms. Most of the time, you will not experience a detailed, vivid memory of your abuse. Your mind is very caring and sensitive to your ability to handle the memories flooding in all at once. The memories will come to you in metaphors, triggers, under hypnosis, PSYCH-K ® session, regression therapy, EMDR, and other models I listed earlier.

Your subconscious mind records your memories, and its function is to store and retrieve data. Your subconscious mind is subjective. It does not think or reason independently. It merely obeys the commands it receives from your conscious mind. The conscious mind is the mind that observes, perceives, and judges its environment. The subconscious mind, on the other hand, is a warehouse of your past. It is always accurate.

The subconscious mind is not creative and does not understand humor, teasing, riddles, jokes. It can, however, remember everything you have ever done, said, or witnessed. The process of recall is allowing the subconscious mind to do its job. You give the order and become open to receive the information in a variety of ways.

As you receive the information, you get to do the work of being curious and interpreting the meaning. If you are like me, at first you will question and minimize almost everything. Alternatively, you may go to the other extreme and *exaggerate* the meaning. The key is not to share your early memories with anyone other than a trusted advisor. You will continue to work with your memories and find the middle ground. Our reaction will cause us to go from one extreme–denial–to another–exaggeration. Do not jump to any conclusions: Get curious and allow the memories to unfold.

Be prepared to find yourself in situations that trigger a feeling or reaction. This response indicates that your mind is attracting the right circumstances to reveal a related memory.

Understanding Your Behaviors— Some Examples from My Life

As you identify situations which trigger a feeling or reaction, you will begin to understand some of your behaviors.

For example, common behaviors I have displayed my entire life are anger and loss of temper. My fight-or-flight response lacked the flight portion of my reaction. I have always been about the fight, which showed up in every sport I have played. Unfortunately, I was taking out my abuse and past trauma on anyone who crossed me.

Since my anger resulted from verbal and physical attacks, I probably should have played tennis or ran track. But no, I played football, basketball, ice hockey, and any other team sport that allowed me to release my aggression on others.

Sports were an automatic trigger. At that time, I thought I was just an angry person. I mean, come on, my mom died when I was a kid! I am sure that is part of it but not the whole of it. After being repeatedly attacked my entire life, the court, field, or ice replicated those events. I was hot-headed, yet I would only engage in a fight when someone attacked me.

As I think back, however, I realize I knew exactly how to push people's buttons to get them to snap, which then gave me cause to go into fight mode. The catch was that each time I would get into a scuffle, I would leave the game and beat myself up. I felt terrible. I was feeling the shame of my action and guilt for taking it out on the innocent. I hated who I was and had no idea how to change it.

The humiliation of my abuse was expressed through self-punishment. As shown in this journal sketch, I am punching myself, banging on the windows, and hitting my head on the wall. I could not fight or scream, therefore I silently took out my feelings on myself.

Playing sports provided key behaviors to identify the truth of my past. I was famous for getting injuries; the significant scrapes and bruises displayed my toughness and spoke to my need for empathy and sympathy. People felt sorry for me. My internal pain was more manageable to express through external injuries. At the time of my sports injuries, I didn't recall the aftermath of my abuse encounters. When my perpetrators would finish their acts upon me, I would harm myself. I would use a tennis racket, my fists, trophies, statues, or anything in reach I could use to beat myself. I would usually pound my legs and torso. I would also find a wall, window, door, or concrete to punch. Keep in mind I was approximately three years old when my self-abuse began.

Another example of behavior revealed to me that I understood later is related to my sister and me. As I mentioned, we had a huge family, which required us to share bedrooms, and sometimes share beds. My sister and I grew up in the same room until we were in high school.

One particular memory was truly revealing for me in my healing process. My father would visit our room late in the evening, time and time again. I would remain awake until I saw him approach the bed. My little mind made up the story that my sister would not survive the endless encounters of abuse. I loved my sister and wanted to save her. I believed I was strong enough for both of us and volunteered myself to my father. It was an act of love and sacrifice.

Ironically, my sister told me later in life that her interpretation of my father's relationship with me was one of preferential treatment and love; my father's favoritism of me scarred her. Here I thought I was her hero, and the selection process damaged her. One of my biggest triggers is being scared. Abuse is scary and will trigger hypervigilance. My life was full of fear and the perfect reenactment of my life was my trip to the haunted house. As I relayed in my earlier story, anyone who has experienced abuse has no business going into a haunted house. My rule is never to step foot into a haunted house, again, ever. To this day, I still regret my actions with the zombie actor.

Another example of a triggering situation assisting in my healing occurred when I was a freshman in college. That summer, I came home and worked at a convenience store. The store owner was married and older than me. I enjoyed his company and liked him as my boss. He would talk about his unhappy marriage and how his wife wouldn't have sex with him. Unconsciously, I felt a sense of obligation to take away his loneliness and hurt. I was triggered, which resulted in having sex with him in his van.

During the interaction, I was *beside myself*. I refer to being numb or checked out as *beside myself*. I was in service of my past and to the crappy life of my boss. This act was not for

This journal sketch shows the level of attention required to survive. I was on high alert in order to be prepared for anything. My life was dedicated to being ten steps ahead of everyone else. I was in FIGHT mode most of my life and worked to be resilient in all encounters.

my satisfaction and, frankly, I didn't feel much of anything. I was not in my right mind; I was in my past mind. The response in my thinking, unconsciously, was "take care of your father or other perpetrators as an obligation to your role."

Some might wonder, how can that be a trigger? Some may think I liked him and wanted it. I want to take this time to prove no trigger goes unchallenged by me. At the time of the encounter, I recall so clearly him asking for clarification, "Are you sure? I thought you were a lesbian." I automatically answered him, confirming this is what I wanted. I DIDN'T, but I was in a full-blown trigger. I was running on autopilot and didn't know how to snap out of it.

If this wasn't proof enough to me, it happened again and again–and yet again. The final time proved to be the most significant breakthrough in my healing process. I worked in the Chicagoland area's youth prison system, and I created a social event for the girls' and boys' prisons. We were transporting the girls to the boys' facility. We were teaching social skills, appropriate limits, and boundaries. I know–ironic, right? The director of the girls' youth division was leading the event with me. We chatted and conversed most of the event. Since it was a dance for the youth, he thought it was entirely appropriate to ask me to dance. Sure, what harm could come of it? We innocently danced together as he told me of his unhappy, sexless marriage. BAM! There I went, triggered into obligatory sex. I was to take care of others and sacrifice my limits and boundaries to fulfill my role.

Upon returning to the girls' prison facility, he invited me in for a tour. I knew what *tour* was code for; my trigger, my past program, was now running me. We ended up having a brief encounter in his office. I was very polite and accommodating. I retreated to my car and promptly realized my role had taken over. I was fully aware but powerless over my program. Filled with guilt, shame, regret, judgment, and self-abuse, I slammed my fists into my legs, stomach, and steering wheel while screaming and crying. I felt so young that I didn't even know if I could drive. I was both *the other woman* and in a relationship.

While it was devastating at the time, this encounter was potent and catapulted my healing. I knew I would not do this if something or someone hadn't trained me to do so. By connecting the dots of my behavior, I was finally free to accept the truth of my past, and I was open to uncovering the cause of my actions and reactions in my life.

As I began my journey of healing, I found relationships to be very challenging. I was waiting for them to end–tolerating abuse, manipulation, infidelity (mine and theirs), shame, and guilt, feeling I was never enough for the person. Numerous intimate positions or certain forms of touch triggered me immediately. I want to clarify: my sexual encounters were *vanilla.* There was nothing creative or out of the ordinary. I was playing by the rules of traditional sexual encounters according to society. If I had any *dirty* thoughts outside of the norm, I would relate it to abuse and shame myself for even thinking it. (If this resonates with you, please stay with me through the next book in this series, *Revealing the Edge,* where I will be leading you into the world of sexual creativity, inner expression, and freedom from shame and guilt.)

My relationships were infested with affairs, either by them or me, and breakups every other day. I operated under the assumption that the other shoe would always drop. I had no trust and surely didn't trust myself. My first long-term relationship lasted eleven years. It was fun and crazy; we were young and volatile. During the relationship, I felt like I had to put up with whatever was given to me because that was *as good as it gets*. My partner had around thirty-five affairs in total over the eleven years. I had my fair share, coming in at two.

Why do survivors cheat? Programming! Programming for covert, secretive, risky, random, mysterious, obscure, and spicy sex. My training was for an unconscious or conscious addiction to this form of inner expression. Again, stay tuned for the coming chapters when we will discuss this topic more.

Glimpses from My Journal

I want to share with you some of my journaling processes through the excavation of my memories.

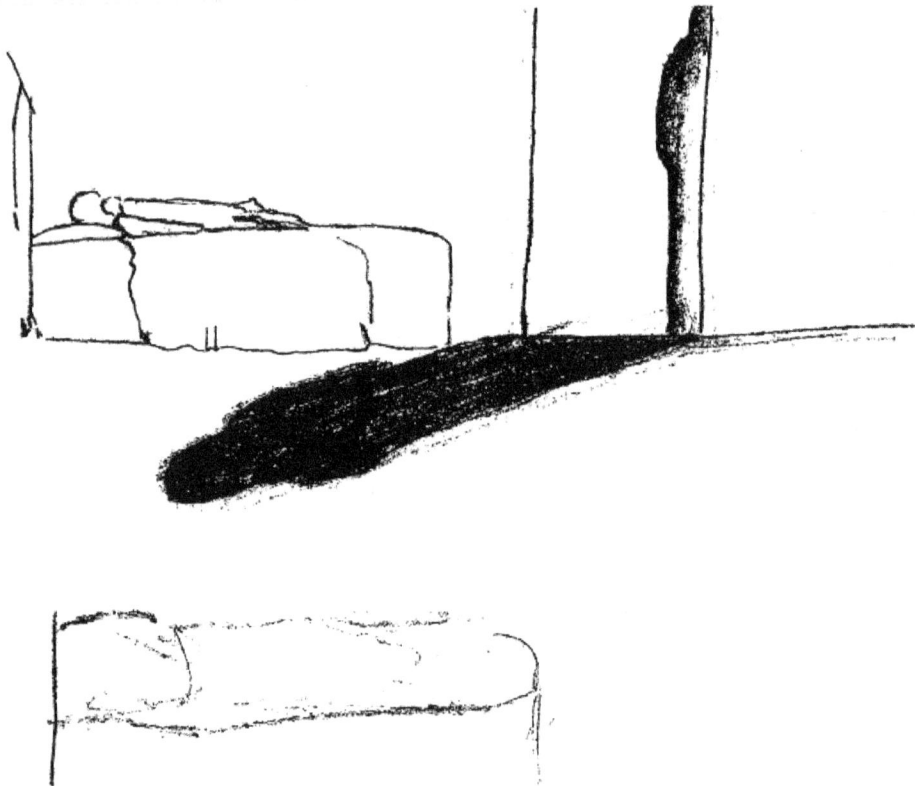

The dark shadow began as far back as my memories go. At the age of three, I can recall the large figure filling the doorway of my room. No matter how still or silent I remained, my fate was known. The process of numbing myself began with the shadow seeping into my room.

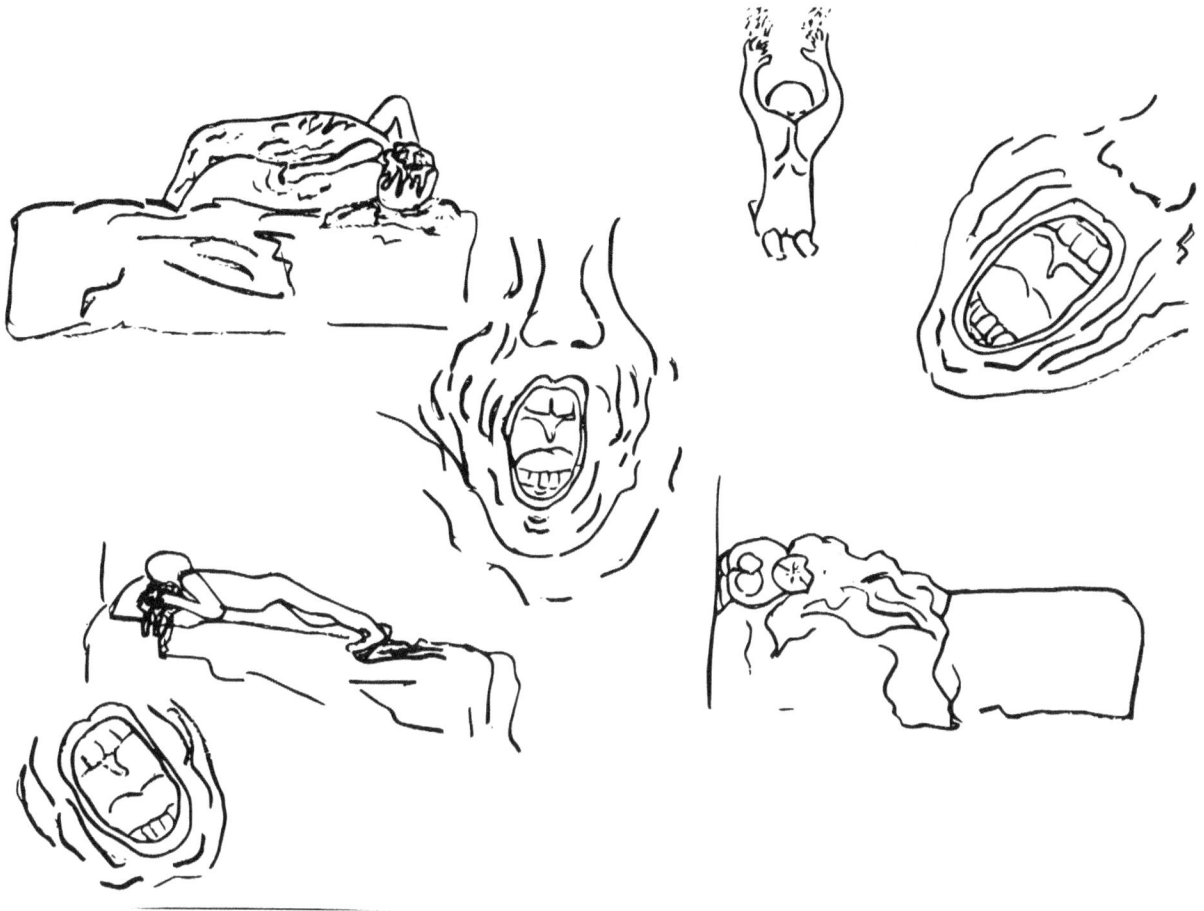

The all too familiar silent scream. The amount of feelings trapped inside of me was incredibly painful.
No escape and no voice, lead to a face of never-ending painful expressions.
The true agony throughout my abuse was the need to suffer in silence.
In therapy, I was unable to let out the faintest sound and release the silent scream.
I worked long and hard to find my voice. Now, you can't shut me up! Mission accomplished.

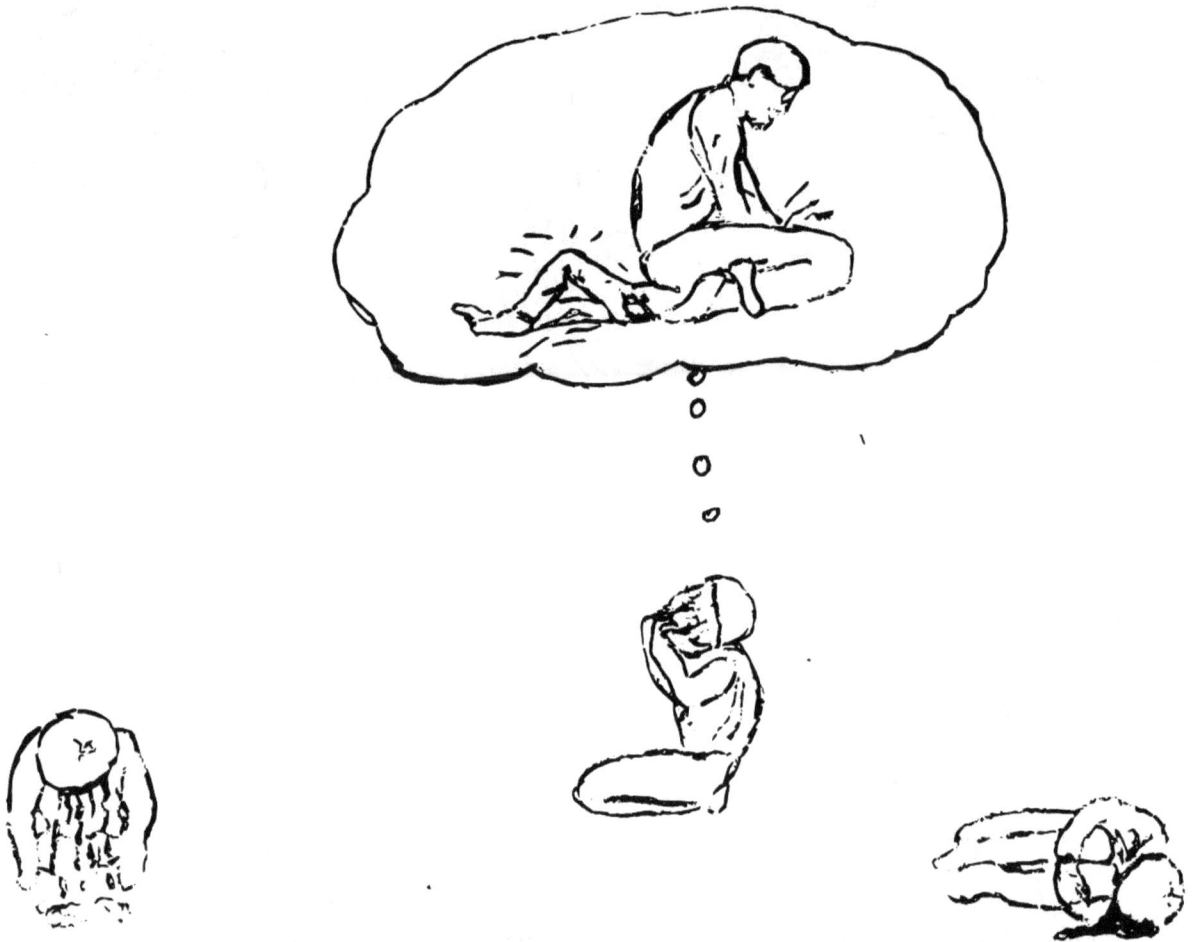

I am truly sorry for the graphic display of my abuse. I am a firm believer in desensitizing
oneself to our abuse, so here it is. Oral sex was a very harsh element of my abuse.
Again, I would have preferred anything but that but it was a regular routine by my abusers.
This sketch shows my never-ending attempts to get the mess off my face.
Clean or not, the effects lasted many years as I felt dirty and unable to clean myself up.
UNTIL NOW!

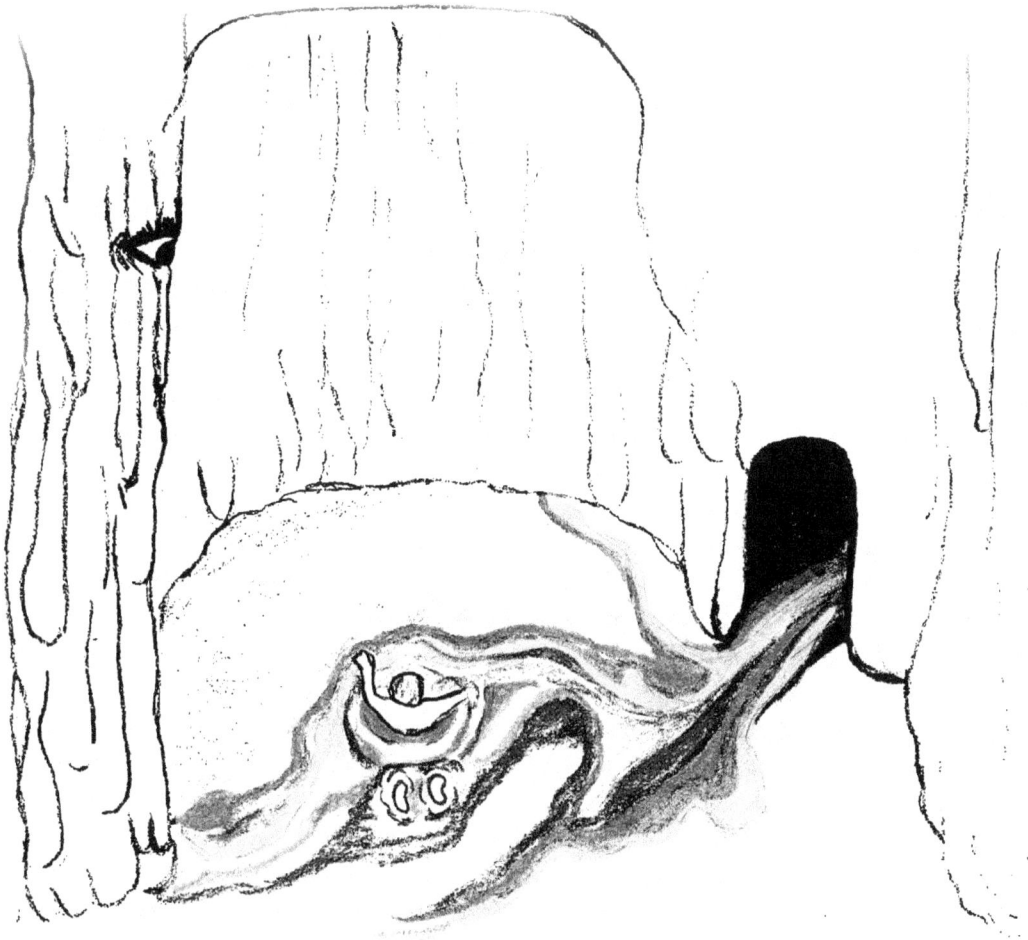

For some, admitting to various forms or acts of abuse and trauma can be very difficult.
I was profoundly ashamed to ever admit to being forced to perform oral sex on my abusers.
I hated the thought of being violated from the neck up. I guess, I was not as skillful at numbing out
that part of my being. This sketch shows the product of oral running down the walls and I am
swimming in the abundance of the aftermath. The color is a stream of healing liquid
washing me clean of the mess made on my face and body.

This sketch is key to my healing. I began my inner child(ren) work and found I was hiding out from the world. I called it protecting the perimeter. I was never going to allow myself to be hurt ever again. This shows the many obstacles one had to endure to get anywhere close to me.

As I revealed more of my inner child(ren), I discovered there were many damaged parts of me. This shows the number of inner children who were extremely damaged. The torture and pain they experienced caused them to go underground. Please do not underestimate the power of inner child work. You will feel CRAZY and like you have multiple personalities.
You will find putting Humpty Dumpty
back together again is easier the more you understand your parts or personality
traits that have developed as a result of your trauma.

"I was beside myself" or "I don't feel like I am in my body"; these are phrases to describe this journal sketch. I never felt whole. I was constantly separated from myself in order to endure the pain and suffering, both emotionally and physically. I would consistently do everything I could to heal myself by imagining wrapping myself in bandages and soothing that part of me.

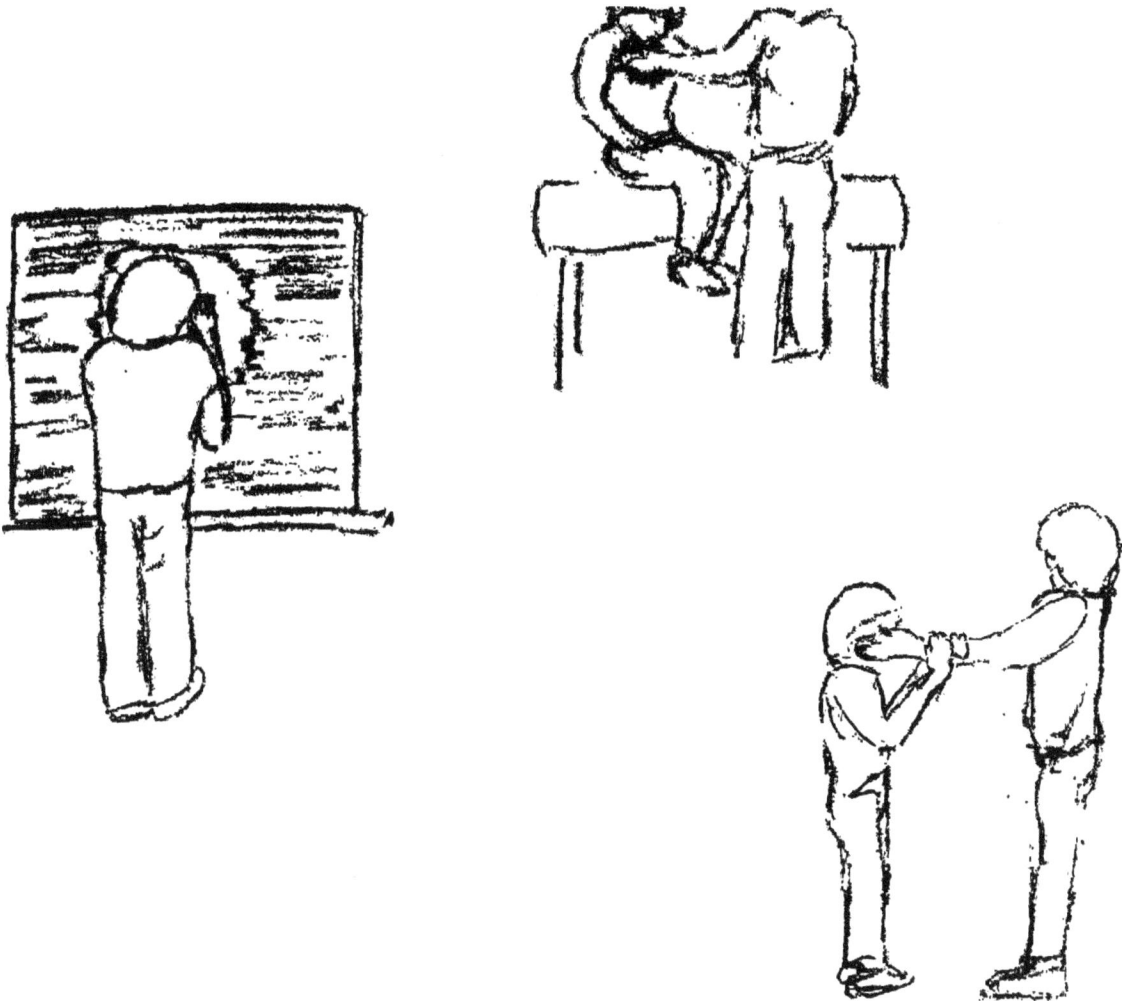

Another example of not feeling whole. Trauma and abuse create a void in your system. I felt my heart was ripped out day after day. The sketch shows my inner child looking inside of my heart to learn what is needed to heal. The other two are images of my higher self-healing my inner child.

These are all sketches of my many kids roaming around the streets of my system. My inner children ranged in ages from months old to 16. Additionally, I had inner adults who were either there to heal the younger ones or had their own issues to heal.

Sam was very instrumental in my healing. You can see from the drawings she was active, a fighter, thinker, and feeler. Savanah was my sweet little one who just wanted to be loved. She was given a new home with my mother who cuddles her in the Spiritual realm. JW was the teen struggling with the identity of being fat, dumb, and stupid.

Savanah

Sam F.

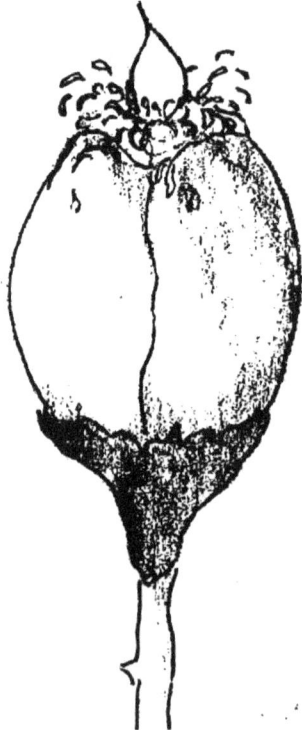

Divinity

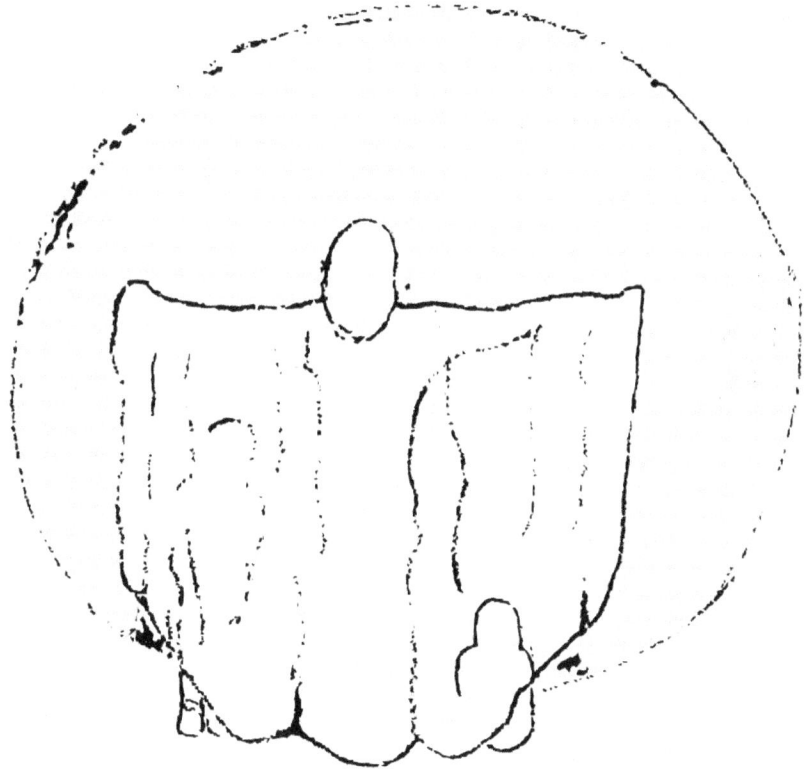

This is a wonderful demonstration of my high self-protecting and healing my little ones.
If you look closely, you can see the outline of them. My higher self, Divinity, was the saving grace
in my life. I struggled to find God, Spirit, or Source to trust and count on. So, I found my higher
self and bridged the gap between her and my higher power/guides/God.

Intimacy, love it or hate it, you gotta have it. I was intimate but not connected for years in my adult life. I discovered my view of intimacy explained my need to be guarded. This image shows you just how awful my view of being close was in my life. I literally felt disconnected. I was not in touch with my body while in my heart. Intimacy was nothing shy of a life in a prison or dungeon. Ice cold, as you see in the sketch.

"Born perfect, programmed to fail."

– Unknown

We are all here for a reason, to make a difference. You were born perfect, and the circumstances of your life may have programmed you to fail. For years, I longed to live on a mountain top. I would daydream about being away from the world in silence. I claimed to become a monk in my dream and vowed never to deal with *all of this* again. It is both a pleasant and unrealistic idea; who's to say it would be easier? If I were to climb my mountain and isolate myself, I would not be of service to my purpose; we are not born to hide. I stand firm on the idea that I lived through what I did to make a difference.

You too have a purpose. You have a reason for all you lived through. My goal is to support you in bringing to life your true nature.

The Dark Night of the Soul

Dark Night of the Soul

Fevered with love's anxiety,
I went, none seeing me
Forth from my house, where all things quiet be

As we move through the healing process, especially the memory phase, there is a definite possibility one will experience what I call a dark night of the soul. Inspired by this poem of St. John of the Cross, the "Dark Night of the Soul" narrates the journey of the soul to mystical union with God. Darkness represents the fact that the destination, God, is unknowable.

In my experience, the dark night of the soul refers to a spiritual depression or detox one must go through to evolve or transform fully. This stage in your life when personal development is inevitable, and you undergo a significant transition to a more in-depth perception of life and your purpose in it, can be caused by difficult circumstances or a decision to step into an enhanced awareness of self. The dark night is often followed by a releasing or shedding of the world as you know it. By letting go of the old, such as an identity, role, relationship, career, addiction, or belief system, it is time for you to give new meaning and set intentions for your life.

During the dark night of the soul, we struggle with our sense of meaning, purpose, and role in the world. Since our lives can feel purposeless and hopeless, courage and trust are required of us to emerge from the dark. The past will strongly tempt us to give in and return to the old.

At any time throughout your healing, you can stop. However, let me warn you: once you break through the denial, you can never go back and be the same person after revealing your desire for more. Fitting into your old life will be extremely uncomfortable, like trying to fit into a pair of size five jeans when you wear a seven. You may be able to zip up those size five jeans or button them, then struggle to breathe, bend, sit, or squat down. Similarly, your life would be dreadfully restricted if you shut down and return to your old ways. You can pull it off, but the level of discomfort is ridiculous.

The allure of victimhood, comfort, and avoidance can be powerful at this stage of your process. Our familiar past is easy; we know what to expect. We need to overcome the addiction to past feelings and programs. During the dark night of the soul, we experience intense feelings of sadness, frustration, hopelessness, meaninglessness, and defeat.

To make changes in our lives, we are either pulled by a dream or pushed by fear. We desire more, and when life is not showing us more, we feel plagued with disappointment and longing. To live a new life, you must experience a shedding of the old beyond your past. I will share a couple of stories that illustrate how we must go through struggles to thrive.

I am sure you are familiar with the story of the butterfly struggle. In short, a little boy was intrigued by the process of a caterpillar emerging from a cocoon to become a butterfly. In watching this process, the boy was worried about the butterfly, who couldn't seem to free itself from the cocoon, so he decided he had to help. He quickly got a pair of scissors, snipped the cocoon to make the hole wider, and the butterfly quickly emerged! Through his well-meaning actions, however, the boy removed the resistance that would allow the butterfly to strengthen so it was deformed and unable to fly. The little boy soon learned that the butterfly needed strengthening by emerging through the cocoon's tight exit before it could fly.

Like that butterfly, all of us require resistance and struggle to give us the strength to fly. Life has pushed us around, and we continue to develop a sense of power and courage to endure whatever we experience.

Another great example is the story of the trees in Biosphere 2. In the late '80s and early '90s, scientists constructed a research facility in Arizona called Biosphere 2. They built the structure to study the interaction between life systems in a controlled environment, to let nature run its course. A funny thing happened with the trees in Biosphere 2, however. Researchers found they grew quickly in this space and then fell over before they were of reproductive age. Why were Biosphere 2 trees such pushovers?

No wind!

The scientists thought they had prepped the environment in Biosphere 2 to reflect nature. Instead they learned that trees are unable to be strengthened in the absence of the resistance that wind provides. The wind is essential for creating hearty trees! As you go through the dark night of the soul, you are becoming more assertive, you are building your endurance, and you are revealing your peace. Your life without storms would be like Biosphere 2.

You are here for a reason, and your work with the dark night of the soul (the space between who you were and who you will become) will allow you to emerge from the darkness into the light. You will have to completely let go of your old self to embrace a more enlightened self. When you abandon your old self, you will enter the darkness where the *old you* will be released, and the *new you* will be designed.

Be aware you will feel very low, almost depressed, during this time of transition as it is a complete surrender. You are grieving the old you. It may not feel like it while you are in the midst of it, but ultimately you will emerge far better than how you were when you went in.

The first step is to surrender and allow the process to unfold. This step is challenging, as you will feel abandoned. You will feel Source/God/Spirit/Higher Power, whatever you believe in or don't believe in, has forgotten you. Feeling alone, you experience a miserable emptiness that leaves you feeling cut off from your life force. This sense of isolation is what the darkness is all about. Aren't you excited to get started?!

I know it doesn't sound fun but trust me. It is worth every tear- and gut-wrenching emotion you experience.

Keep in mind that in the darkness during this first step, you will call into question everything you ever believed about life. The very makeup of who you are as a person will fall. As a result, you will feel confused, bewildered, angry, desperate, helpless, and hopeless. AND– just when you can't handle anymore, the pieces will all start to make sense. Upon your awareness, your sense of self will be cast a new light. You will begin to see, feel, imagine, and believe in new possibilities. You will be ready to reprogram a new YOU!

Dark Night of the Soul Steps:

First, begin asking yourself a series of questions:

1. Why am I here?
2. Why me?
3. Who am I?
4. What is my go-to emotion?

5. What memory is the most painful for me to recall?

6. What's missing from my life?

7. What do I believe to be real about me?

Here is a sample of my *Dark Night of the Soul* work. Feel free to use a chart like this to help guide you through the process. Find a safe, quiet place where you will not be disturbed and make sure you have a box of tissues by your side. Play music, if you wish. Be gentle with yourself and begin to shed the old by writing your *Elements of the Dark Night*. After you have a list, create a new one on the right describing what you learned from these elements. Please keep a copy of this list as it is powerful and helps you move into a deeper state of permanent healing.

Elements of the Dark Night	Learning
1. Guilt and shame	1. The most compassion to have is for me.
2. Distance and turmoil in my relationships	2. Every act is a cry for love or an expression of love, no matter how unskillful. My actions were a cry for "love," one that is a true love. The message I got around love was wrong, and I continued to search for that love.
3. Continued self-abuse and disappointment	3. The pattern is up for healing, and I GET to repattern and redefine love. Create love in a healthy, honest way.
4. Self-hatred	4. I have the opportunity to see myself for who I can be and not who I have been up until now.
5. Failure	5. Forgiveness! Forgiving myself for the actions that I did out of what I knew. Given the state of mind I was in, I did my best with the tools and stories I had. I am rewriting the story of my love life.
6. Disgusted with me	6. Determination to stand firm in the face of temptation. Paying attention to what I am paying attention to in my thoughts. Daydreaming of real love, not acting out love.

| 7. Distance and turmoil in my relationships | 7. SAY YES!!! The confusion is a story or a paradigm that will shift through my surrendering to it. Confusion is the smoke and mirror to my truth. |
| | (I swear I am confused just writing that statement.) My subconscious mind will bring me to the clarity of my denial. |

The purpose of creating this list is to completely transform situations, events, and memories in your life. It is to give new meaning to everything. We set up beliefs and patterns based on our past-operating system: based on what they told us, what happened to us, and what they said about us. The dark night method is the best one to destroy, demolish, and collapse our old programming, our system. Once you have completed and worked your list, the dark fades, and now, as it was said, "Let there be light." From the darkness of the old mind, you emerge into a transformed state of consciousness. Life has meaning again!

Since I moved through the *Dark Night of the Soul* work, I now have far more enlightenment and freedom; I know it can and will happen throughout my life. I have had many a dark night and repeated the process.

Make it your goal to continue working on the meaning of your life based on your new learning. Living as a victim is not an option. The dark night of the soul is a death of the egoic sense of self. You get to experience the end of your old self and the birth of your new, authentic self.

CHAPTER 4

Voice of Power

*C*an you keep a secret? Of course, you can! You have been keeping far too many secrets, and now it is time to find your voice of power. We will walk through the next steps of your healing by preparing you to finally let go of the secrets. The concealed memories, truth, secrets, and expectations will be divulged and shared–on your terms. By lifting the veil, we will be revealing your power.

What does the voice of power mean? Great question! You get to decide what that means for you, and how you express your voice. I am not saying you will have to lease a billboard, do a Facebook Live, or write a book, although you could! You get to choose what is your right next step.

There are so many invisible side effects of sexual abuse that most are unaware of in their lives. The key to unlocking those hidden side effects is your voice. Begin to speak up and decide what you would love. As children of abuse, we were put into a dysfunctional system and trained to behave within that system. In my family, I learned on day one that you had no choice and no voice. You could not express your opinion or dissatisfaction about anything, let alone your disgust about what was happening to you. As a result, you remained hidden, not wanting to stand out or take a stance about anything. The best solution for stepping into empowerment is to stand up for yourself and never take a back seat to anyone. It makes me crazy when I see people discounting their own opinion or conceding to others, so they don't make waves.

One of the fundamental issues with unreleased truths is that it becomes our new normal. We have been keeping secrets for so long that we don't even realize we are doing it.

Unfortunately, it leads to various issues on physical, emotional, mental, and spiritual levels.

In this chapter, we'll look at the importance of your voice and how you can find it. I'll share my unusual story of how I found my voice. And I'll describe how I set up a meeting with my abuser and used my voice to aid in my healing. Then we will look at ways you, too, can hold a meeting if, and when you are ready.

Find Your Voice

My goal is to help you speak up. I say, stir it up, make waves, be heard, and be respected for your truth. Let's start by finding your voice, as there is no greater power!

Reveal the secrets to yourself, then begin speaking up. I encourage you to start with a simple "yes" or "no" to questions in your daily life. It can be an easy, "No, I don't want the liver and onions," or "Yes, I would love pizza." (I mean, who would say no to pizza?) I love the saying, "Make your yes be yes and your no be no. No lukewarm." "NO" was not something we ever dreamt of saying to our abusers. When I was seven years old, I tried to say no to my father, and trust me, I never did that again.

When we begin to find our voice in everyday situations, we free the dark secrets that hold us in shame or guilt. I'll share my story so you can see how it worked for me. It includes my thought patterns at the time and a cautionary tale for sharing too much with the wrong person.

My Unique Path to Finding My Voice

In 1985, I started my journey to tell my truth and begin my healing. I attended therapy sessions twice weekly and participated in an AMAC (Adults Molested as Children) group run by Gale Vance from the YMCA in Illinois. During my therapy sessions, I went from having no memories to having far too many memories, from absolute rage to a decisive confrontation. Throughout my healing, my plan to confront the truth changed every step of the way. I wanted to hurt my father and the other perpetrators. In my mind, at that time, there was no better way to express my pain than through revenge. I had numerous methods of revenge planned for them all. It was not going to be pretty.

Luckily, my rational mind talked me out of this solution. Even though I knew I could never go through with any of it, it felt great to imagine the morbid outcome. Not to mention, I just wouldn't do well in prison.

So I masterminded Plan B. I was going to have all of my abusers arrested and tried before a jury of my peers. They would pay for what they had done. Again, my mind talked me out of it by convincing me they would blame me for the entire thing, or worse: I would be called a crazy liar.

While I was brainstorming plans, I decided to confront my abusers. I was determined to speak my truth after years of dedicated work on my healing. I planned to start with my brother and then move to my father. It felt like the path of least resistance.

I set up a meeting with my oldest brother to help design the master plan. Unfortunately, my intentions were made known to the entire family, which resulted in a family meeting (without me) arranged by the perpetrating brother. His purpose for the meeting was for him to inform the rest of the family that I had gone crazy. He claimed he was very concerned about my lack of mental health and my sexual identity crisis. He also informed them of my "sexually deviant behavior" in sleeping with women.

Looking back, I have to give it to him. His plan was genius. He was setting me up to take a fall. My brother told the family that a crazy person in a sexual identity crisis usually accuses someone of sexually abusing them.

Jane,
    This is the Jane I thought
I knew. You have turned Love
into HATE for us all. I now know
how you must feel. I will not hold
this against you, but your lies
will not go unanswered. Some day
we will meet again. All of us
knew of your deviation before
you had the courage to admit it.
I am not your excuse!

After the secret meeting, I received a call from my brother and his wife. They were furious, calling me names and threatening me. My brother declared he was coming over and bringing his hunting rifle and that he was going to kill me. This was a threat I took very seriously; my brother was fighting for his innocence.

I was so afraid at the time, I decided the best course of action was to disappear. So I fled. I moved in with my therapist. Yes, back in the mid-eighties, the rules were not the same as today, and no one thought twice about a patient moving in with their therapist. I lived with her for a few weeks until I found a place of my own in a different city. I went underground for approximately five years, give or take. During that time, I continued my healing journey, building the courage to stand up for myself.

I desired to reemerge powerfully and profoundly. Some of you may have heard of a woman named Oprah Winfrey. Well, after being invited on the show, I thought, what better way to *come out* with my abuse than in front of twelve to thirteen million viewers?

The show's theme was sexual abuse and the entire studio audience, including me, were survivors. There was my face splashed across the global screens, and I was discovered by my family. It was "go time." I was coming back into the fold with a vengeance. I planned to confront the leader of the generational pattern of abuse and dysfunction, my father. My goal was to stop the cycle of abuse in my family and never cower to anyone again.

Understand, you do not have to make the confrontation process part of your healing. There are several factors involved in confronting your abuser(s). I will walk you through my confrontation process and then give you some ideas to consider.

My Meeting

It was Saturday, January 23, 1988, at 11:00 am. As I peered out of the second-story window at St. John Lutheran Church, I could see my father rubbing his hands together as he slowly walked up to the entrance of the rectory. Seeming to be much smaller than I remembered, he appeared weaker, older, and almost frail.

My hands were shaking, and my heart was pounding. I was about to meet my father for the first time in five years and confront him with his actions. He had no idea what I planned to share. You see, my father was happy to blame my brother and everyone else who had abused me. I had not declared my memories of being abused by my father until long after I separated from my family. I could see the resistant excitement in his face. He had waited years to reconnect with me, though for a very different reason than mine.

I invited two of my friends to support me during the confrontation. They were there for both physical and emotional support. When he arrived, I escorted him to the table in the large room. In preparation, I had written a long letter and memorized it. I informed him that this meeting was for me to express myself only. Demanding confirmation that he would not speak or attempt to discuss anything in response to what I was about to share, he agreed, and I proceeded to read the following letter:

Dear Dad,

There are some very important things you need to hear. I want to begin by asking you to allow me a few minutes to speak and tell you what I have to say. I do not want a discussion at this time. I want you to just hear me.

I have been waiting a long time to come out and tell you that I know you sexually abused me as I was growing up. All my life I have suffered with that miserable secret, not being able to tell or ask for help as a child. I need to tell you how that has affected my life and express my feelings.

I want you to know that your sexually abusing me has scarred me very deeply and it will be a memory that I will always have to live with. I wished for years that I was wrong and that my own father would never have wanted to hurt me that way. Unfortunately, I have had to accept the fact that the father I loved violated me and destroyed any trust and love I had. I have carried the burden of your choices and have been feeling the pain of your abuse my entire life. I hurt so badly inside because I truly loved you and trusted you but that trust had been betrayed over and over again.

There are so many things I missed out on as a result of you sexually abusing me. I never knew what a real childhood felt like. My life as a child was taken away from me and I missed out on the joy and freedom a child should experience. My childhood was filled with hurt, pain and deep betrayal. I lived a life of confusion and mistrust. It has been hard for me to accept the fact that my own father that I trusted violated me and shattered any hopes or dreams for a happy life. I trusted you as I grew up and loved you very deeply. I believed that the way in which you loved me was honest and not wrong. I thought everyone's love was like that, only to come to realize that love has limits and boundaries, and mine were greatly overstepped. I hurt so deeply because I did not have a childhood. I had to grow up so quickly not only because mom was an alcoholic but because you were sexually using me as an adult. I feel such anger and rage inside because I deserved so much better. Like any other child I deserved honest love and attention, not to be violated and used. I was a very special child and you missed out on that part of me.

I am very angry that my life has taken this course, I am angry at you for not taking the responsibility as an adult and setting limits and protecting me from your actions. My anger towards you has been so great at times. I have denied that I had any other feelings towards you because of the deep pain that lives inside of me. I did not want to admit I loved you because the betrayal and hurt is so great. I will always feel the loss of a father's nurturing, honest love.

As a result of your abuse I have struggled with feelings of not being okay, being dirty, guilty, ashamed, unloved, rejected, hurt, confused and like a victim. You never thought of me, the choice was never mine. You never considered what it would do to me and how greatly it would affect my life. You only thought of yourself.

I have made the choice to confront you because I will not carry the burden of your choice ever again, it is now yours to carry. I will accept the fact that you abused me for your reasons alone, not because of something I did.

I resent you because your choices interfered with you being my father. A father that could have taught me how to be financially efficient, professionally marketable, and confident. I was only taught how to please people and compromise myself. I resent the fact that I had to learn all that on my own. In addition, I missed out on advanced educational and vocational opportunities because of my obligation to pay off my undergraduate work and therapy.

I have struggled financially for years attempting to pay for therapy and undo what has been done to me against my will. I have been scarred very deeply and have committed a great deal of time sorting out the pieces of my life and allowing myself to have a life of health and happiness, something I have never felt before. I resent you greatly each time I put out another sum of money to pay what you did to me. It angers me to carry the responsibility of your actions.

My life has been very tough and I have lived with

Page 3

the consequences of being sexually abused. I do know there will always be a part of me that knows the pain and sadness I have lived through and I will never forget the sorrow and grief I feel, but I will not let it hold me back. I will continue to grow and not be a victim any longer. I will be free and continue on with my life experiencing it at its fullest potential. I have established a wonderful, successful life of love and happiness. A life I truly deserve. I am no longer a victim, I am a survivor.

At this time dad, I am only willing to accept an apology from you, otherwise I will say goodbye.

Jane, your daughter

I was so nervous and scared throughout the entire process, and when I finished reading the letter, I asked him to leave. He promptly stood and walked out sobbing. Finally, I began to breathe again.

I would love to tell you the confrontation gave me the absolute freedom I was seeking. It didn't. After all the work and preparation, I felt guilty and my system began to unravel. I started to doubt my memories and signs of my abuse. I argued with God for a different past, and a part of me wanted to take it all back. This reaction is natural in the confrontation process, whether the abuser speaks to you or not. Crazy, I know!

My right next step was to release the past and forget about my abuser. I knew I was to continue therapy and on the path of healing, no matter what my father did from that point forward. You may be as shocked as I was when I tell you that I received a letter in the mail from my father. He sent an apology letter confessing his actions. It was surreal!

Dear Jane   Feb 25

   I wrote you a letter on the 12th but on re reading it I found that it rambled and got to involved in my stuff. What I have to say is short and is from the bottom of my heart.

   . I have been very sad these past weeks knowing now that I have been the cause of your sexual abuse. It is from the depths of my very being that I come to you in all my love and apologize for what I have done to you. I am very sorry to have hurt you in this way and can only ask that you accept my apology knowing that it comes to you with all my love.

   I pray for you and for myself that we both may be healed of this very deep hurt each in our own way. My feeling for you is one of love and caring that you will grow and prosper in spite of the terrible thing that have happened to you.

May you feel my love for you as it crys out for your happiness.

With all my love
Dad

Again, I wish his confession was the answer I needed to reveal my missing peace. It wasn't. I thought this apology was what I needed. I realized this missing peace was not about my abuser; it was about me. I could not gather enough justice in my life to fill the void. I needed far more, and no one on the outside could make me whole.

As it turns out, while I thought I needed to reveal the missing peace, NOTHING was missing! The answer was in me and it had been all along. Yes, the answer was inside of me the whole time. I simply had no idea how to reveal it. As a result, I committed to continue on my mission for a life not run by my past.

I took advantage of my father's willingness to participate in my healing. If anyone had told me that this man would serve as one of the most significant people in my recovery, I would have called you crazy. Yet, he was. Over the next three decades, before my father died in 2015, he was instrumental in my growth and power process. For that, I am eternally grateful. Trust me, it took more than two of those decades to arrive at this point of gratitude.

I enrolled him in my healing and had the freedom to communicate just about anything I felt to him. I am a feeler and became a very clear communicator. I wasn't always very skillful in the articulation of my feelings as I progressed through my therapy. However, I was very talented at using many very colorful phrases, words, names, and attacks. One might say I had a sharp tongue. My father put up with hours of screaming, yelling, name-calling, and rejection. Rightfully so, given what I felt he took from me. It was the least he could do, and he did.

You might be shocked to learn I gave the eulogy at his funeral. Okay, I only delivered his eulogy because I didn't want anyone getting up and telling the mourners what a wonderful man he was. I made it crystal clear that he had some serious faults and a few good qualities.

Confronting my father was the best thing I ever did. In contrast, I never confronted my brother or any other abusers. I was profoundly aware the work I was doing from that point on would be alone.

Confronting Your Abuser(s)

If you consider confronting your abuser(s), allow me to share a few steps to follow.

Step 1: WHY? First and foremost, you must understand why you want to confront them. If you have an attachment to the outcome, I highly recommend you do not do it. I believe the time for confrontation is when you intend to share your truth and story, to voice your power further. You must do it without an expectation of the response.

My goal in confronting my father was to get my story out. I was determined to speak my truth with confidence and conviction. I never in my wildest dreams ever imagined he would confess and apologize. It was a byproduct of the confrontation; it was never my intention.

Step 2: Stand Strong. You must feel confident and unwavering in your story. Be sure you are solid in your stance so you can calmly and confidently overcome any objections to the truth. The best place to be, emotionally, is neutral.

My confrontation was an exception to the rule. I know many survivors whose efforts to confront have harmed them. I believe I was fortunate to have had the response I did with my father. I am sure I would have been in danger from the other abusers.

I was not neutral; I tend to be a person of immediate action. I don't know how to marinate and think about much for too long. If you are also a mover, just know you must be able to stand firm and strong.

Step 3: Prepare! I highly recommend you write out everything you want to say to your abuser. I like to call this a "data dump," as I mentioned when we discussed journaling earlier. Simply start by writing anything that comes to mind. Get it all out, and do not filter any words or thoughts. Feeling free to express yourself is a significant part of the confrontation process.

You will likely not share everything you have written and that's okay. After you have written out what you would love to say, edit your writing, and create a carefully crafted message that is to the point and leaves nothing open to interpretation. State the facts, feelings, and intentions.

Refrain from using words such as:

- sorta
- kinda
- things
- stuff
- might

Stand firm in using phrases like:

- I know
- I am
- The fact is
- You did
- As a result

Leave no room for rebuttal or discussion. The confrontation is for you to get out in the open about what happened and how you feel about it. Keep in mind, you do not intend to get a calculated response from them.

Step 4: Practice and Rehearse. Memorize the information you are going to share. If you have a structure and all the points laid out in your mind, there is less of a chance for you to waver. By memorizing and reading the letter to them, you will stay on track and be less emotionally engaged. You do not want to be processing feelings while confronting.

Please know I am not saying, "don't feel anything." While you are speaking, you will feel crazy. I am, however, suggesting you talk in a more business-like and professional manner. The confrontation is not the time to open yourself up to emotional vulnerability.

Our response to stress is fight or flight. During the encounter, you want to be firm and direct, and choose to fight. This situation is one in which I highly recommend you shut down your emotions. The time for feeling is when you finish.

Step 5: Support. Gather your support team and prepare them with precisely what you want them to do for you. Ask them to be there for you before, during, and after the meeting. Select your team wisely. You need people who believe and support you fully.

Each person needs to be clear on their role, and they need to be clear on what you need during the confrontation. I told my supporters I wanted safety first; I didn't want to feel threatened in any way.

I laid out the logistics ahead of time. Before we started, I directed my supporters on where to stand during the meeting, how long to allow it to go on, and clear directions for the aftermath. My other request was to hold a space for me to be in my power. I did this by asking them to see me as strong and firm.

Step 6: The Invitation. You can send the invitation in a variety of ways. You can email, text, call, write a letter, or maybe have someone close to your abuser invite them to meet with you.

I didn't prepare my father for the meeting. I stated I wanted to share a few things with him. Frankly, I was afraid he wouldn't show. The risk was worth it to me, even though I knew I was blindsiding him. I was willing to ambush him in order to have the chance to meet. A part of me believes that he must have known. My father was fully aware of the family meeting about my sexual identity crisis that my brother arranged, for heaven's sake. Either way, I was willing to call a blind meeting.

You must decide what is best for you and your safest plan of action during the confrontation. Focus on you and your safety. Do not be surprised if the perpetrators don't show; those who are well aware of their actions do not want to be exposed.

Step 7: Rules of Engagement. You call the shots because setting firm limits is vital in your healing. There were no boundaries during the abuse. Now is the time to be clear and expressive on what is okay and not okay.

Stand firm in your expectations with no guilt or question. You may want your abuser to only listen and not say anything. This was the best way for me to execute the process with my father. You can decide if and when you permit them to speak.

Do not allow them to defend or deny. Be prepared to end the meeting at any time you decide. Remain calm and neutral.

Set your boundaries and clear expectations by stating what your relationship or actions will look like moving forward. Think about what, if anything, you need from the person, and communicate your expectations. Leave nothing unsaid.

Step 8: Celebrate. You have completed one of the most important meetings of your life. Be proud of yourself. You will also want to express gratitude for the person, your support team, and how far you have come. This accomplishment is no easy task and is worthy of a celebration.

Confrontation is not for everyone, and it is not necessary to heal and grow. The missing peace is in you, not in those who abused you.

CHAPTER 5

Inheritance: Programs and Patterns

Curly hair, eye color, freckles, dimples, free or attached earlobes, and lips are just a few of the observable physical traits we inherit from our parents. Remember in science class when we learned about DNA and how our collective traits are coded or inherited?

The basis of the age-old argument of nature or nurture is how we inherit our characteristics and acquire them from our environment. Are we the way we are because we were born this way, or did we develop into who we are because of our upbringing?

Nature is what we often refer to as our pre-wiring and is influenced by genetic inheritance and other biological factors. Nurture is our traits influenced by external factors and is the product of exposure, life experiences, and learning.

Some of our reactions are acquired habits and patterns of behavior. We will identify those we developed due to our abuse and the environment that perpetuated the dysfunctional behaviors. Identifying these traits will enable us to recognize them in ourselves, and begin to control our responses to them. This crucial step brings us closer to becoming a survivOR.

Traits from My Past

When I was growing up, I had no clue that the way I responded to my experiences had anything to do with my abuse. I attributed it solely to my family's gene pool. I observed my seven siblings reacting and behaving in a particular way to their environment, and I followed suit throughout my life.

I learned and acquired my meaning of love from my family. Love was secretive, covert, and isolated. My father expected this expression of love, and I was programmed to please and behave. I never fought off my abusers because I had no idea it was wrong. This behavior was our "language of love."

It was not until I was about six that I began to question the ongoing abuse apart from my father. Remember, I was trained from birth to accept that this type of behavior was love. The change came about when my brother began abusing me. That was different. I could tell that this abuse was not from a language of love, and instead was a demand for attention. So, I was not as cooperative; I resisted, which resulted in more force and violence.

As I write this, I think back to how I felt when I would attempt to fight. In my mind, I felt more physically capable of fighting off my perpetrators than I was. While I felt like a giant, I was a child at that time; I was always tiny in reality. All three of my brothers looked like men at the age of sixteen years old, with facial hair, and they'd maxed out their height by that age. Even though I didn't have a chance, I continued to make every attempt to fight my brother.

With my father, I never tried to fight him until one night. I decided to run and hide downstairs in the family room. I crouched behind the chair, breathless. I was determined to escape just this one night. I believed I was as invisible as I was a giant; however, he discovered me in no time. Silently, I was given the message never to try hiding again. And I didn't.

Awareness of Your Actions

If anyone you know makes statements similar to "I am who I am," this is a clue that there is a program running. Their past is running them and they are unaware or unwilling to change. They have come to accept their behavior as their norm. The fact that you are still reading this book demonstrates you know who you are and are willing to change.

My goal is to create an awareness for you of your actions. I want to do that by outlining the various acquired traits resulting from abuse. Know that you will have your characteristics and behaviors. Many are unconscious patterns of behavior or triggers you have grown accustomed to in your life. By staying mindful and aware of your conditioned response, you can identify your triggers. You may not even know the underlying programs; we will dive into them as we go.

1. **Hypervigilance:** Hypervigilance is a state of increased alertness. In this state, you're extremely sensitive to everything. It can make you feel like you're alert to any hidden dangers, whether from other people or the environment. You are jumpy with fast reflexes and have immediate knee-jerk reactions to your environment. For example, you may overreact if you hear a loud bang or misunderstand what someone says to you.

While these dangers are not real, we react as if they are due to our abuse. When you are in constant high alert, your body and mind work overtime to keep you safe. Being on guard is entirely understandable, given your past. Abuse results in fear, and we are masters of the fight-or-flight response.

For me, darkness means danger. When the lights went out in my house, bad things happened. That left me in a state of fear and hypervigilance for most of my life. I remember when I spent the night at a friend's house in high school. When it was time for lights out, she pulled down both the room-darkening blind and curtain in the window to ensure not a sliver of light would get in. I thought I had gone blind. As I began to panic, I felt a rush of anxiety and a great fear of danger lurking. AND–there was no danger. I was not at home, so I was not in danger, and my friend's house was safe and sound with no abuse. However, my mind reacted to the darkness, not the reality of the situation.

Hypervigilance can be utterly exhausting. It can also interfere with interpersonal relationships, your work in the world, and your ability to be fully present in your daily life. Since your past is running you, you are not free to create an intentional future, and this will be an overarching theme in your everyday life.

As you learn about how the various patterns and programs impact you, you will begin to see just how super alert you are to the world, inside and out. You will be shocked at the amount of observing you do every day, even if you think you are not very observant.

2. **Lack of Trust:** Trust is earned and developed over time in any relationship. If you grew up in an environment of abuse, you had no reason to trust. Every time someone abused you, they breached your trust. As a result, learning to trust can be a very long road.

There is always a question in the back of your mind, unconsciously, and you are unwilling to be truly vulnerable in your relationships with a lack of trust. You may tend to question the authentic motives in all your relationships. What do they truly want from me? Are they looking for more? What are they hiding from me? When will the other shoe drop? You have one eye open at all times. Why wouldn't you? Your past trained you to guard yourself for anything.

Without trust, having good relationships is impossible. You may have a relationship or two in which you are displaying trust issues. As I look back on my relationships, I can see that I was engaged and connected, with a readiness to leave or be left. In other words, I was ready at a moment's notice to survive another betrayal, so I was looking for what was wrong and never appreciating what was right. Ironically, I found each of my relationships to be what I imagined. AND I overstayed my welcome.

As I shared earlier, I was in an eleven-year relationship directly out of college, riddled with affairs, both mine and my partner's. Cheating was my way of avoiding intimacy and connection. While the secretive encounters hurt me, it felt familiar to me, and I believed this relationship was the best I would get. My view of life kept me in a dysfunctional relationship as I always recreated my childhood of betrayal, pain, and abuse.

On the flip side of no trust, there is blind trust, which might resonate for you as it does for Denise. She confesses to always being too trusting of people growing up and even in adulthood. As children, it is natural to view our parents as the authority on all things in life. Heck, often we have no other point of reference. Our parents are supposed to teach us right from wrong, good from bad, and how to maneuver life.

While Denise didn't have much of a trustworthy relationship with her mother, she had an overly-trusting relationship with her father. The result? She found herself trusting men but not women. She always had more male friends in high school, college, and even into adulthood simply because she blindly trusted them. Unfortunately, not every man deserved to be trusted, and for her, it resulted in being taken advantage of mentally, emotionally, and physically. Denise's father produced her deep-seated training.

3. **Lack of Limits and Boundaries, or Having Way Too Many:** Rules, rules, and more rules. I have set up more of them in my life than you'll find in a courtroom. I also like to call them "very clear limits" and "boundaries," an expression of your physical, emotional, and mental thresholds established to protect yourself from being manipulated, used, or violated by others.

If you don't speak up, you sacrifice your desires. Setting clear limits and boundaries honors who you are and what you think and feel. It is how we define our individuality. Communicating your boundaries takes out the guesswork for you and others. It prevents anyone from having to read your mind, hope they are meeting your needs, and accidentally overstep.

If we had known how to set boundaries in the first place, we might not have experienced the abuse. Instead, we learned that abuse was the natural way of life in the family. Our inability to say "yes" or "no" is linked directly with our need to seek approval from others, which is how we survived our abuse. As victims of abuse, we sought favor from our abuser to feel special, loved, or accepted. As children, we did not have mature enough minds to reason out the long-term effects of abuse. Our training was on how to act and never to fight it. Does that mean we wanted it? GOD NO!!! It means they prepared us very well to fall into the trap of abuse.

The absence of limits and boundaries may have been the norm in your family home as it was in mine, where nothing was sacred. Family members would barge unannounced into the bathroom during a shower; there was no sense of privacy or dignity. They wore my clothes, played with my toys, violated my personal space, and overachieved at harmful teasing.

In contrast, my current boundaries are very apparent, so I am assured that my interactions and relationships are mutually respectful, appropriate, and caring. Learning to say "yes" and "no" is vital to our healing.

I would love to say I began setting up my limits and boundaries with a gentle yet firm voice. Nope, I was very unskillful, angry, aggressive, and short with others. I thought I had to come on strong since I had no frame of reference, and no one had ever respected my boundaries. OH, and the fact I had no self-esteem didn't help. I didn't feel worthy and therefore I believed no one would honor my requests.

When I recognized my lack of control over my personal space and my need to please others, I asked myself questions to help uncover and reveal how I wanted to express and set my boundaries. If you are not sure you are good at setting boundaries or don't have any at all, ask yourself these questions:

- Is it easy for me to speak up when people are making decisions?
- Who are the people to whom I am afraid to say no?
- How often do I care about what others think?
- Am I afraid of disappointing others?
- Do I feel guilty putting myself first?

- Do I often feel my actions are selfish?
- Do people clearly understand my rules of engaging with me?
- Am I deserving of respect by everyone?
- When was the last time I said "yes" when I truly wanted to say "no"?
- Is it easy for me to vote on plans or significant decisions?

Understanding your desires, dreams, wants, needs, and rules are vital to you standing in your power. You can set boundaries for your personal space, emotional needs and desires, thoughts, physical possessions, time, energy, culture, religion, and sexuality. When you set limits, you confidently support a healthy sense of self, confidence, and worthiness. You preserve your energy and no longer give away your power. The best part of making up your own rules is you are the center of your Universe. It is time to become independent and leave codependence behind.

The key to excellent communication in any situation is to take personal responsibility for your actions and reactions. Sharing clear boundaries with others creates good relationships.

Here is a list of statements you can use in a relationship to help you set a boundary or expectation and establish good communication between you.

1. What I would love to do is teach you something about me.

   When you do/speak/act _____, I feel _____.

   What I would prefer is _____

2. Let me help you understand me a bit better.

   When you do/speak/act _____, I feel _____.

   What I would prefer is _____.

3. Help me learn more about you.

   When I do/speak/act _____, you feel _____.

   What would you prefer?

4. Help me understand you better.

   When I do/speak/act _____, you feel _____.

   What would you prefer?

Using these statements has saved many of my relationships from complete misunderstandings and miscommunication. I highly recommend you memorize them and have them handy during any conversation.

You can also use a standby phrase used in any therapy session, "What I heard you say was _____."

This form of active listening is the best way to honor and reflect another in conversation. Rehearse and practice these statements for the best communication skills possible.

4. **The Blame Game:** Taking personal responsibility may prove to be a challenging part of your journey. It was for me. I didn't have a say in the manner I was treated while I was growing up. None of the abuse was my fault, nor was it my choice. I knew exactly where to direct the blame with all the details to persecute the perpetrators. As I began my healing process, I was determined to make them all pay. My life was a constant struggle with anger driving me, and my default was to blame.

Don't get me wrong; your abuser is to blame for the aftermath. They are not the cause of your continued struggle. I adopted the statement early on: *If you were raised in a family like mine you would be*_____ (insert consequence or failure here).

One time, I was told by a dear friend with tears in his eyes that I was placed about seven miles behind the starting line in life. I felt like my abuse and my crazy family cheated me, stifled my success. I would use blame as my excuse for not having, being, doing, or experiencing something or anything. I didn't take responsibility for my life until I realized the power my abuse had over me.

Shifting the blame onto someone else can be a subtle way to attack them. We might be holding a grudge against our abuser(s) or someone for something they did or said. We reflect on how we were wronged or hurt and look to our past experiences for the blame. We have enough burdens dealing with our past, so why not put the blame where it belongs? The reason is it robs you of true healing. When you shift the blame onto someone or something else, it is the perfect way to remain unaware and avoid having to do a deep dive into feelings, actions, and behavior patterns. This approach maintains a state of perpetual pain and victimhood. I look at my past and chuckle at the amount of blaming and grudge-holding I did.

You are NOW responsible for your having, being, doing, and experiencing. Yes, it sucks that you experienced trauma; the real injustice is you not living life on your terms. If you continue to live from the past through blame and lack forgiveness (ugh, the F-bomb), you will continue to give your power to the past.

Blaming is a great way to shift responsibility. When you own your part in a situation, you call the shots; that is your power! My brilliant therapist, Dr. Dina Evan, told me that *in my vulnerability is my power*. I thought, are you kidding me? That is when I am at the most risk. I continued to examine that statement and found that if I confessed my thoughts, feelings, and actions, I could move forward on my terms. I tested the theory, and I encourage you to do the same.

Here is how it works. Let's say you are like me and have a particular way of eating. Before gluten-free, vegan, Keto, Celiac's disease, and other food movements and diets were well-known, I was very precise about my food. When some of us were at a restaurant, I would order with numerous stipulations. Some of my friends would make fun of me. Before my new experiment–in my vulnerability is my power–it would mortify me when they noticed that I asked for special orders when we went out to eat.

I decided to experiment with this vulnerability theory. Before I would head out to dinner with my friends, I would announce to them, "If anyone has a confidence issue around my special ordering at the restaurant, you might reconsider joining." I added that I would only dine with accepting, open individuals. Do you know, after making my statement, not one of them said a word? Not one! During previous outings, I was the butt of teasing. Now I realized I was onto something. I began to state my truth and preferences, boldly and directly. To this day, most everyone knows how I am feeling, what I prefer, and more importantly, how I feel about them. That mantra was and is still my most empowering statement. Give it a try.

I will refer to the first boundaries statement a few pages back and fill in the blanks. It might sound something like this: What I would love to do is teach you something about me. When I order my food at a restaurant, I am particular about my preferences. If this is an issue for you, I suggest we pass on dinner. If not, great. You will be so surprised by how many people support you. If they don't, guess what? They are the wrong people for your circle.

Many times, as survivors, we are attracted to or pick people who support or mirror our past. These people and their behaviors are familiar and draw our minds to them like a magnet. However, we are working to create a new standard and new habits as a result. Personal responsibility is a way to stand fully in your power. Set yourself up to win. Speak your truth, set your limits, and take the blame. It is the fastest path to healing.

5. **Fight or Flight:** First described by Walter Bradford Cannon, the fight-or-flight response (also called the acute stress response, hyperarousal, or the Crumbles) is a physiological reaction to a perceived survival threat.

I am sure you are familiar with the fight-or-or flight response. I believe each of us is inclined to one or the other. In the event of a perceived threat, I am ready to fight, quick to react, immediately jump into action; I will stand up and defend myself, verbally, or physically. My instinct is to lean into the threat rather than run from danger. This proactivity can include *stranger danger* or simple miscommunication. It is not always my preferred knee-jerk reaction, although it seems to be a natural uncensored response.

Unconsciously, I turned my fight into drive. My energy equivalent is that of five humans. I could do the work of ten in half the time and get three times the results. Indeed, I loved to drive in all areas of my life. I was programmed to compete, win, and accept any challenge to emerge victorious. I was either working hard or playing hard.

Others are flighters (is that even a word? Let's make it one!). At the onset of a threat, flighters are off to the races, avoiding danger by fleeing. Like a deer in the forest, flighters don't charge and look to defeat their predator. They are running to safety. For Denise, the minute there was even a hint of conflict or threat, away she goes, either physically or emotionally. She would do anything to avoid any level of confrontation. She is a bit better now, but it is still her default.

Are you aware if you are a fighter or a flighter? Neither is right or wrong; what is important is to fully understand whether your trigger is fight or flight. Know that your abuse heightens the flight-or-flight mechanism, meaning you get stuck in the hyperarousal state, similar to hypervigilance.

If you have unresolved emotional distress or face ongoing life stress, your body stays in a perpetual state of fight or flight. This tension taxes your sympathetic nervous system and can result in harmful side effects. It is important to retrain your mind to a calm state of ease using mindfulness and breathing to determine the actual threat level. Since you have an overactive mind, you have a hasty reaction.

The fight-or-flight response is a natural safety mechanism. The problem is that as survivors, we tend to stay in one or the other. Trust me, most people live in one of these states due to constant demands. Picture the daily responses of a single mother of three, one with special needs, a demanding career, a household to run, a dating life, care of elderly parents, soccer games to attend, meals to be made, laundry to be done, homework to do, and bills to pay. This tangle of elements causes us to be our *first responder*, so we run around doing far too much with far too little time for self-care. As a result, we are ON all the time.

In this state, when you encounter a perceived threat such as a screeching car or a dog rushing at you, your hypothalamus, a tiny region at your brain's base, sets off an alarm system in your body. Next, your adrenal glands fire off a nerve and a potent hormonal cocktail made up of adrenaline and cortisol. I know this formula well due to all the years I was told I had adrenal fatigue.

While you are reading this page, you may be thinking about your own sense of drive. Perhaps you have gotten great reviews and feedback, even been applauded for being so driven. The world celebrates and admires a multitasker. You may even take pride in doing it *all*. People around you know if they want something done, they can go to you. Great for your career, but hard living is not so great for your mind, body, spirit, and healing.

Your natural stress response–fight or flight–is meant to be utilized occasionally and within reason. If you are driving yourself every day and tackling never-ending demands, your body is unable to self-regulate. Being addicted to the rush of adrenaline and functioning best under pressure requires you to have a continuous stream of adrenaline in your system. Your body never fully returns to normal, to drop your hormone levels back to a state of calm. Your heart rate and blood pressure are unable to remain at baseline levels, and everything else is on high alert because you always feel under attack most of the time, although it's not necessarily real.

I had no idea I was feeding my fight response every day by fearing loss, lack, or failure. I lived with this tremendous fear of losing everything, which drove me to keep gathering more money and more stuff. I was addicted to worry and fear, which ultimately was all about security. While fear was my primary motivator in my life, I had no idea I was in a perpetual state of a fight-or-flight reaction.

Our bodies are amazing. They can repair, adjust, and adapt to so many things. When you become mindful of how you respond, you can live in a less stressful, more energetic frame of mind. Please understand that while everyone has the potential for similar reactions in life, whether fight or flight, hypervigilance, or lack of limits and boundaries they will not have it to the same degree. Abuse has a way of preparing us for the worst in life. Our work is to take what happened to us and create a best-case scenario future.

CHAPTER 6

Victory Over Shame and Guilt

"Shame is the lie someone told you about yourself."

–Anais Nin

"Guilt: the gift that keeps on giving."

–Erma Bombeck

Two more patterns and programs we inherited due to our abuse and trauma are shame and guilt. What's the difference? Shame is an unpleasant self-conscious emotion typically associated with a negative evaluation of oneself, usually resulting in a sense of worthlessness. Shame also triggers feelings of being defective, unacceptable, even damaged beyond repair. Guilt is a specific reaction to a transgression and is an emotional experience. The voice of shame says, "I am bad," or, "There is something wrong with me." Guilt speaks with, "I did something bad." I don't know about you; I confuse the two all the time.

The abuse you lived through resulted in multiple conflicting feelings unconsciously running through your mind. Knowingly or not, you are victim to those feelings and stories. When left unexpressed, they perpetuate a sense of shame and guilt. As a survivOR, you will pay constant attention to effectively navigating these emotions without getting stuck in the feelings too long. The important fact is you must verbalize them to a partner, spouse, friend, or therapist. My entire philosophy is based on finding the voice, which includes giving feelings the freedom to flow.

However, in my experience, most people don't always pay attention to the feelings and emotions that come up for them in their life. Instead, they "stuff" their feelings, as the saying goes. The purpose of our feelings and emotions is to be felt, expressed, and transformed. If we don't get the feelings out, they will find a way, either becoming internal or external spillage. Sigmund Freud said, "Unexpressed emotions will never die. They are buried alive and will come forth later in uglier ways."

The Insidious Nature of Shame and Guilt

Shame and guilt can be lethal when you keep them hidden. The power of shame increases when you stuff it inside of yourself and never release it. Shame is like a big giant beach ball you are attempting to hold underwater: it is going to pop up. When you begin to speak the truth, shame is released and rendered powerless in your life; it cannot survive exposure.

Throughout my healing process, I felt an excessive amount of shame and guilt. I blamed myself for the abuse and anything else that went wrong in my life. Keeping the secret and remaining silent promoted feelings of shame. Also, the stigmatizing nature of sexual abuse and fears about how others may respond is traumatic. As memories of the abuse surface, there is an awareness that sexual acts you experienced are considered wrong and dirty. This feeling of shame eats away at you and holds you back from sharing with anyone.

As more memories bubbled up in me, I began to feel a sense of embarrassment and guilt. I was disgusted by the actions and felt a sense of responsibility. I was ashamed about what happened to me even though I had no choice. I believe when remembering as an adult, it triggers you to see things from that perspective. As an adult, I would not be abused in this way, ever. My mind was unable to separate the two circumstances; I experienced abuse as a child, and now, as an adult, I understood what it meant. Therefore, I felt a strong sense of humiliation and disgust at myself for not stopping the abuse. My guilt grew as I revealed more and more details.

This emotional distress continued to play out in my everyday life. I was self-critical, far too hard on myself, and nothing I did was ever good enough. It was all because of what happened to me, which was outside of my power. No matter how many times I heard the words, "It's not your fault," I still blamed myself in some way for being submissive, weak, or a wimp.

Explaining Specialitis

There is another aspect of shame and guilt. I know I must address it, even though many find it to be too triggering. So, here it goes. A part of you may have felt a level of fulfillment, satisfaction, pleasure, or that you were special as a result of your abuse. This concept was the worst one I ever heard during my therapy! I was repulsed and devastated by the mere thought of enjoying the way they treated me. It triggered a flood of unbearable shame and guilt in me. Even as I rejected the idea, I was privately investigating the accusation. It was going to be my little secret for life. Well, at least it was going to be my secret until I decided to write this book.

I will admit that my abuse created in me a feeling of being special. My abusers chose me over my siblings, which meant there was something about me that stood out. For me, this belief grew into a lifelong struggle with what I call *Specialitis.*

I use this term, *Specialitis,* to describe my constant need to be the favorite one. I have been competitive for a long time to stand out in my life and career. It has been exhausting, and talk about shame and guilt; it took me out of my power. I depended on others to prove to me that I am worthy. Physical touch is a basic human need, and especially as children, we naturally desire and need nurturing affection. During your abuse, you may have enjoyed feeling special, loved, or chosen in ways that you reject now.

I studied the Romanian Baby Phenomena[2] in junior high and learned about how important physical touch is for emotional development. In the late 1980s, there was an increase in the Romanian orphanage population. The caregivers at the orphanages could not care for all the babies, so the only physical touch they received was when they were being changed or fed. Starved for attention, the little ones would rhythmically bang their heads against the cribs for stimulation. They also would stare at their hands, seeking any form of connection. There were lists upon lists of problems these children suffered as a result of this neglect, ranging from poor impulse control, social withdrawal, inability to cope and regulate emotions, low self-esteem, poor intellectual functioning, and low academic achievement. When I studied the Romanian Baby Phenomena, I was profoundly aware of why I felt so lost and alone. I was metaphorically banging my head against the wall seeking appropriate stimulation.

---

[2] https://www.latimes.com/archives/la-xpm-1990-12-10-mn-4673-story.html

All I knew was that my abuse served as my physical connection, which is why it feels satisfying and pleasing at times. Our bodies naturally desire physical pleasure and stimulation. As noted in the study, we crave it, and the sensation of touch results in a positive association, whether we know any different or not.

"There's Something Wrong With Me"

Other forms of shame and guilt make it challenging to overcome the adverse effects of harmful childhood experiences. These feelings can go too far, go on too long, and prevent us from relating to others in healthy ways. For many, intense and long-term shame seems to be an unshakable part of life. The experience of being manipulated, used, exploited, and harmed as you were can lead to a feeling that there's something fundamentally wrong with you. Many take on the abuser's responsibility; you may believe that you brought on the abuse, and it could be what your abuser told you.

Even being unable to connect to memories of abuse, Denise was shocked by how many older men she attracted during her teenage years and 20s. She could never figure it out; she didn't flirt, act out, or do anything for the attention. She has never been one to enjoy the spotlight on herself. If you are questioning your memories or lack thereof, the clue is in observing your relationship patterns. For example, you may believe for no apparent reason that your permanently tainted presence has less value than others. You may become disillusioned with who you are and worry about anyone finding out; if you are genuinely fearful that someone will see the REAL you, this reaction is what I call the Imposter Syndrome on steroids.

Imposter Syndrome

Have you ever felt afraid to say or do something for fear that someone will call you a fraud? If so, you have experienced imposter syndrome.

[3]Impostor Syndrome (also known as impostor phenomenon or fraud syndrome) was coined in 1978 by clinical psychologists Dr. Pauline R. Clance and Dr. Suzanne A. Imes. It refers to individuals marked by an inability to internalize their accomplishments and a persistent fear of being exposed as a "fraud." Despite their competence, those exhibiting

---

3 Clance, Dr. Pauline R. and Suzanne A. Imes. "The Imposter Phenomenon in High Achieving Women: Dynamics and Therapeutic Intervention." *Psychotherapy Theory, Research and Practice* 15.3 (1978)

the syndrome remain convinced they are fakes and do not deserve the success they have achieved. When you point out their signs of success, they dismiss them as luck, timing, or deceiving others into thinking they are more intelligent and competent than they believe themselves to be.

Someone who feels like an imposter identifies with statements such as: "I hope they don't find out who or how I am because they will leave," and, "I'm afraid they'll discover I am innately flawed, dirty, or broken."

On your way to becoming a survivOR, you will likely struggle with Imposter Syndrome. Giving in means you end up in a never-ending battle to disarm your doubts and fears. What is it, specifically, that you're afraid people will find out about you? I swear to you, I kept referring to this THING people would find out about me, although I could never identify it. What if it is because there is nothing and never was anything to find out? What if we were so good at carrying the abuser's shame and guilt, we lost sight of who we are? What if the time we spent on hiding that THING was an illusion?

It is not easy to break it to you: We have indeed wasted a boatload of time worrying and hiding out for fear of being discovered. The abuse we experienced did not flaw us. I get it! That part of us can be persistent and wants to hide. The best way to overcome Imposter Syndrome is to identify specific doubts. What are you afraid of? Write down those doubts and fears here:

I am afraid:

_____

I doubt that I can:

_____

More thoughts I repeatedly say to myself:

_____

You may find these thought patterns are preventing you from moving forward and doing new things, and they are likely showing up in your relationships. If you continue being plagued by your self-sabotaging thoughts and fears, they will keep you distant, hold you back during all of your interactions, and produce more feelings of shame and guilt. You may appear real and confident, while the effort on the inside to keep you safe is alive and kicking.

I know. I would show up to events or parties and people would see me as confident, competent, and assertive. Everything on the outside looked great, and meanwhile, the inside was working overtime protecting our little secret–that THING.

Religious Influence

Another influencer that will produce guilt and shame is religion. To be clear, I do not have an opinion one way or another if you are religious. While I do believe in a power greater than myself, I do not think there is a power that judges, condemns, or crucifies me for my actions, thoughts, beliefs, or expressions. I am more of a spiritual person and live by the laws of life and love.

If your upbringing was religious and you experienced sexual abuse, you have likely experienced great conflict. Why? First and foremost, you have held a terrible secret about your abuse, and you are fighting the paradox of sin.

In general, coming out about your sexual abuse is more readily supported now in our society. In contrast, if you come out about your religious struggles or shattered faith, this is considered to be unacceptable. Leaving a community or religion can mean losing everything when your upbringing is filled with religious rules and dogma.

Remember that you may feel conflicted even if you grew up in a moderately religious home as I did. It is all about what your mind does with the message: the directives to "inspire" people to do better and be better. By convincing people, they will forever need to ask for forgiveness, these religions profess that the only way to save yourself is to submit to the rules and admit you are a sinner.

While we are growing up, we don't fully understand the ideology of being a sinner. It may feel like an inquisition and pick away at our self-esteem. Religion can be baffling to any child, let alone one who is experiencing sexual abuse. You are trying to be a good kid and obey your parents, yet it makes no sense. The result is usually shame and guilt.

When you hold back your emotions, all you feel is shame and guilt continually running in the background each day. As a result, you will never feel whole. Living in a body with so much suppressed emotion is quite uncomfortable. Even when you think you have fooled yourself, that you have overcome these memories by ignoring them or pushing them to the side, they will continue to fester deep within you, gnawing at you from the inside out.

Stuffed feelings have adverse internal effects on your system, and they will show up in the outside world. These unexpressed feelings and emotions can limit you by impeding your relationships, stealing your joy, destroying your vitality, robbing you of your inner peace, and taking you out of your power. Most of the time you don't even know it; inside, you are like a ticking time bomb. One day, your emotions can explode and wreak havoc in your life.

Feelings of shame and guilt can be excruciating, especially when we have never fully allowed ourselves to feel them. Once we allow that to happen, we discover it is not our feelings that hurt us but rather the denial of them that causes us the most pain.

Shame and guilt are significant hurdles in the healing process. You may not be aware of feeling anything positive from your abuse, and that's okay. It's time to get curious and open to the possibility that your body and heart were seeking natural fulfillment. If you feel shame, guilt, or embarrassment resulting from your discoveries, keep reading, because we will work on releasing this very soon.

OR survive OR PEACE

Our entire journey has brought us to this point, and now it is time to decide. You can survive *OR* live in peace. Peace is never again feeling like something is missing or innately wrong with you. Peace is knowing you are fully worthy of all you desire in life. Fill your *OR* life with every vision and dream you can imagine. How do you earn peace in your life? I am so glad you asked.

"There is a single mental move you can make which, in a millisecond, will solve enormous problems for you. It has the potential to improve almost any personal or business situation you will ever encounter, and it could literally propel you down the path to incredible success. We have a name for this magic mental activity. It is called **DECISION**." Bob Proctor begins his book, *Decision,* with this concept. We are going to launch an *OR* life by making a single mental move. Ready?

CHAPTER 7

Put a Stop to Victimhood

Why me?
Not again!
The other shoe always drops.
When it rains, it pours! There isn't enough time.

"**I** am NOT a victim." You say it all the time, and in doing so, you know and affirm that you are a surviv*OR*. Yet what if unknowingly, you occasionally slip into the role of victim? I'll tell you a secret: Everyone does it–without even knowing they've done it.

No matter the cause or degree of your abuse or trauma, being a victim sucks. On the other hand, being a victim or taking on the victim's role can bring us wanted attention. For example, we learned as kids that if we skinned our knee, and someone was putting Bactine on our wound, we received sympathy, and our pain was validated.

Any level of attention in victim mode, however, reinforces our abuse. The goal is to stop seeking attention by not asking for it. Let's put a stop to victimhood and find our voice to draw the desired attention we need. We start this process with a better understanding of the victim mode.

There is a difference between being a victim and having a victim mentality. I encourage you to commit to discovering if and when you are playing the *poor me* or *victim* card.

I get it. There are times I would love for someone to rescue me or feel sorry for me. Long ago, when I was very unskillful at asking for my needs to be met, I played the victim's role instead of speaking up.

My friend, Abbie, was very clear about her need to be a victim. Whenever she felt sorry for herself, she would ask her partner to say, "You poor thing." She even gave that voice a name, Iris, so her partner could call Iris out.

What is the *victim mentality*? It is the belief that one is always a victim: the idea that bad things will continually happen to one.

Let's look at how the victim mentality shows up in the world:

1. **Why me? Why is it always me?** Are there times that it feels like the whole world is out to get you? And you wonder to yourself why everything seems to work out for others and not you? You may be singularly focused on yourself and your pain, and also ask "why me?" about your abuse.

There are going to be times when it seems like nothing is going your way. However, listen to the comments you make, like, "What happened to me is_____," and "Just when I get back on my feet, someone or something pulls the rug out from under me." Consider how you set yourself up as a victim of circumstance, rather than someone who controls their life and emotion. Does this hit home for you?

1. **Not my fault; if they would have** or **hadn't; Look what you did to me!**
   Victims express these declarations often. It is vital to stop blaming others, and that includes your abuser(s).

For many years, I used the abuse card, feeling sorry for myself or as an excuse for behavior. I would argue for my failures, shortcomings, lack, or circumstances. My most incredible line of all times was, "If you grew up in a family like mine, you would also be_____." You fill in the blank. It worked for so many different situations! I was a master at spinning the responsibility onto others.

Come now, you know you're with me on this. We learned early on to survive, and we blamed others because we had to take the pressure off of ourselves. Unfortunately, this approach provides only temporary relief from pain, leading to feelings of powerlessness and hopelessness. The million-dollar question is: What is your role in any situation? Does life happen to you or by you?

2. ***Poor pitiful me! I always have to be the strong, responsible one! At times, it would be nice for someone to take care of me!***

When you continually feel that you lack the power, resources, and willingness to take back control, your desire or ability to solve a problem or cope effectively with situations feels pointless or daunting. Things pile up and you believe you are the only one who cares or can carry the load. It might feel a bit like you are the sacrificial lamb. You sacrifice so much for others and your situation, yet things are just out of your control.

Victim mentality is a need for control and self-preservation. Abuse and trauma left us powerless, and we had no control over our environment, body, mind, and circumstances. It was a disaster and extremely damaging. When we experience powerlessness, we manifest it, and to combat that feeling, all we want is to control and feel protected. **"Nobody likes me, everybody hates me, I think I'll eat some worms."** My mother used to recite this song to me when I was whining or playing the victim. First and foremost, what a terrible expression! Although, I guess if we are begging to be a victim, it is like eating worms.

If you are often afraid people are upset at you, or you have done something to offend or hurt them, you are running a victim program. You are skillful at convincing yourself you can "read" other people and are positive they are upset, disappointed, or angry with you. The majority of the time, this is false proof they are against you, and therefore these inaccurate feelings are why you feel bad. You tend to think others are purposefully trying to hurt you.

Also, deep down, you expect others to read your mind. I mean, come on, you think you know how others feel about you, so you, in turn, expect them to understand how you feel, too, right? If you can read minds, why can't they?

It is a terrible habit to expect others to know how you feel. It is a sign of your avoidance to engage in heart-to-heart communication, which will help you take responsibility for situations.

3. ***If Anything Can Go Wrong It Will Go Wrong! AKA Murphy's Law!*** This supposed law of nature has also been called Karma. Whatever you call it, victims perceive problems as catastrophes. In the victim mentality, you are on the lookout for the other shoe to drop, so you tend to exaggerate your concerns. You are ready to one-up anyone or any situation.

I have observed one-up-man-ship in the world of surviv*OR*s. One person shares their abuse story and the next response is a bigger and better story. I had someone say to me, "My abuse was far worse than yours ever could have been."

This statement is a cry to be heard and validated. Notice "who" is speaking when you listen to someone talk, whether it is a friend or a person walking by on the street. If it isn't the mom, the dad, the kid, the car, the job, or the dog, it is something. That something is a desperate cry of the victim mentality.

4. ***Excuses!*** Having excuses is a primary sign that someone is operating from their victim mentality, and creative ones are an attempt to minimize responsibility and assign blame. Apologetic reasons dress up rationalization, defensiveness, and justification.

Do any of these excuses sound familiar?

- I'm too old, too young, too tall, too short, too fat, too skinny
- I'm not educated enough
- No money, no time
- I just don't know the right people
- I've been there, done that, and it doesn't work
- I'm not confident enough
- I lack experience, knowledge, and resources
- I'm just not ready yet
- No clue where to begin
- It's just too difficult
- Not good enough.
- I just don't have any luck
- It never seems to be the right time
- What will others think?
- I'm afraid of making a mistake
- I just can't deal with all these problems

The art and science of excuse-making are no different than overcoming sales objections in my coaching business. While excuses are great reasons, sounding convincing and legit, they are rarely the real reason, and are always deflections from the truth. Excuses dodge commitment and obligation. They also support keeping you stuck.

I love excuses! After all, they help us feel much better about ourselves because we avoid being exposed and keep expectations low. Not to mention, we win the sympathy of others.

Excuses are great protectors, too. They provide us with valid reasons to help us explain away why we just aren't good enough.

*   *   *

With these examples, you understand what I am getting at when it comes to playing the victim. It is a result of our training and a means by which we survived. It is exhausting to think of having to take responsibility for everything, and overwhelming, especially at a young age. The best and only way for us to survive was to deflect the burden of life onto others.

I love it when I slip into my victim. I make comments such as, "Why do I have to do everything?" and, "No, don't worry about it, I will do it all." My all-time favorite go-to victim card is referencing anything around my childhood. I know there is no way anyone will refuse to feel sorry for me due to my background. It is a sure-fire way to get attention, validation, love, and protection; it is also a manipulation. Today, it needs to end. Forever. While my commitment to follow through on this declaration is not easy, it is doable.

What does your victim card look and sound like? Understand that it is not IF you are playing the victim card; it is WHEN. We all know it, and while we are experts for a good reason at acting within our victim mentality, it does not serve us anymore.

When you need compassion, pity, support, love, or help, just say so. Avoid the quiet epidemic of self-loathing and self-destruction. Remaining a victim or operating with a victim mentality is a classic form of self-sabotage, which I am sure you have heard about before. I feel compelled to elaborate on it.

Self-Sabotage

Self-sabotage is a common habit for most people, and survivORs are overachievers at it. The most well-known self-sabotaging behaviors include procrastination, addiction, dependence on drugs or alcohol, comfort eating, playing the victim, and forms of self-injury.

Another way to sabotage yourself is to shut down and not speak your truth. Denise sabotaged herself as a victim for years and never realized it. She put off essential tasks, chose self-medication over consulting a medical professional, consumed prescription drugs and alcohol, stayed quiet, and did not stand up for herself. She could never say no and always stepped up to help anyone with anything. Now you may think, good for her;

however, it was all for the wrong reasons. Are you like Denise, a victim to prioritizing the needs of everyone else? Have you removed yourself from the equation?

Sabotaging behaviors often go unnoticed, and too many are unaware they are doing them. This behavior is a result of the programs running in our subconscious mind. I can sum up self-sabotage with two words: self-talk.

Every message of doubt and fear that runs through your mind will produce self-sabotage. Over the decades, people I have worked with will find every reason, aka excuse, in the book to justify why they did or didn't do something. They will say, "I am so busy at work, my mother needed me, the kids stressed me out," or any other reason to justify things not getting done. It isn't true. So what is the truth?

Rewiring Your Programs

To replace self-sabotage, let's look at the programs running you and how we can rewire them. We will strengthen your confidence by interrupting ingrained patterns of thought and waking up the cycle of the mind.

Disappointment: In addition to betrayal, we also experienced epic disappointment, one of the worst feelings. We will avoid these feelings at all costs, so we want to control any disaster before it strikes. I like to call this approach to life "protecting the perimeter," a way to safeguard your emotions and the consequences of your circumstances. While protecting yourself is smart and practical, it is best not to do so at your expense or your relationships.

Remaining a Victim: Choosing to stay in the victim mode guarantees distance in relationships due to deep-seated trust issues. Abuse is a means of victimization, which means that each event anchored the belief and program "I AM a victim" in your mind, so it became a part of your standard operating procedures embedded in your brain.

I lived for years as an unconscious victim. I had a habit of making people wrong, so I could be right, pointing out flaws or reasons why others were less than me. Finding fault and having a negative filter allowed me to feel better about myself.

The only reason bullies do bullying is because they feel less about themselves. To feel better, they put others down, tease, beat, and annoy. While I wasn't a bully, I found reasons to feel better by keeping the light off of me and shining it onto others' faults.

If you are operating from a victim mentality, you will talk about others more than yourself. Victims are continually seeking proof that others are untrustworthy. It is a defense mechanism or a system in hypervigilance. Time spent talking about others far surpasses the amount of time the victim spends on being confident.

If a victim does talk about themselves, it will begin with, "You won't believe what happened to me," and inevitably will veer into blaming others or talking about others. When you are in victim mode you talk about events for a long time after the fact. You can't wait to tell a friend or two about the terrible luck you had, or even better: the awful thing "so-n-so" did to you. You run the same situation by all your friends and anyone else who will listen.

How People Make You Feel: Listen up as this is a vital topic: as humans, we are continually feeling emotions; however, there is not a single person on the planet who has the power to make you feel something or anything. That's right! Their behavior, actions, or words may trigger feelings, which trigger memories of similar events. You go into survival mode, and the past feelings flood into the present situation. You then look for the root cause *outside* of yourself or someone to blame. Why? Because that is so much easier than looking at yourself! Remember: YOU decide whether and what you feel or not. I am going to tell you the truth. When I feel like crap, I will start to blame someone, anyone, for my crappy day. I always laugh when I confess this from stage when I'm speaking to an audience. I encourage people to blame others when you feel like you can't get over yourself. I preface it by explaining that in the Alcoholics Anonymous (AA), Narcotics Anonymous (NA), and other A worlds, blaming is a big no-no. Maybe in your world, too, yet I am still doing it.

However, I use a different theory around blaming than most. You may know the AA expression, "when I point the finger at someone else, three fingers are pointing back at me." So, I use my entire hand instead, so all of my digits are pointing and blaming.

When we look outside of ourselves to find the source of our myriad of emotions–happiness, sadness, anger, gratitude, jealousy, and so many others–we give our power away.

Never give anyone the power to *make* you feel something you don't choose to feel. Controlling our emotions is our decision. It may not feel that way because our triggers and programs often hijack us.

If we are at the mercy of someone or something outside of us to make us happy, we are in for a huge surprise. Emotions determine our state of mind. We get to choose how we feel, no matter what happens in the outer world. I have the choice to think, "Yes, it was terrible of my father to say those things. What I did with them was my choice."

I was utterly relieved the minute someone introduced the concept of owning my feelings. Knowing that no one has the power to make me feel a specific way, I am bulletproof. Okay, not so much bulletproof as aware. The hardest thing to do during a triggering conversation is to halt emotions and reflect on old feelings. Yet that is what you need to do to move out of the victim mindset and into your power.

Spot It: Begin to listen for your hot buttons or triggers. Have you heard of the saying by Martha Beck, *"You spot it, you've got it"*? I first heard about this concept in addictions when I was working at Lovelton Drug and Alcohol Treatment Center (a facility which is no longer in operation).

Whenever you have strong reactions to a person, situation, or action, your response points to something that you possess within yourself. "You spot it, you've got it" occurs when you get irritated, annoyed, sad, or depressed by the behavior of others. In other words, what I hate the most in you is likely what I hate the most in me. When we react to anything, it is because there is something within us that we need to heal and release. It is necessary to raise your self-awareness and understanding of the "you spot it, you've got it" concept so you can reduce blind spots in your system.

How do you use this technique to help you "spot it"? Whenever you encounter someone, envision yourself holding up an enormous mirror facing you. Our outer world is a reflection of our inner world. Each person and each situation is an opportunity for us to learn something about ourselves, move through it, and heal. For example, if you often experience aggressive behavior from others and are triggered by it, then there's a good chance that "you've got it."

My "spot it" is when I am with others who will not speak up for themselves and take action. My frustration peaks when I am coaching a client, or a friend for that matter, who stays in a victim mindset, arguing for lack, struggle, brokenness, less than, or unworthiness. It drives me crazy. I witness how they take it personally and spiral into victimhood. Then, I pause, look in the mirror, and reflect on what in me needs to be healed, released, or forgiven. That pause brings us to our next rewiring process.

Power of the Pause: When you reflect in the pause, you grow and evolve the most. That was when I realized what triggers me and understood why I was doing most everything in my life while afraid.

I have befriended my fear because it was not going away. I have been on my own since my mother died. My dad would travel for weeks on end, leaving my sister and me at home alone. I was afraid to be alone at night, and navigating day-to-day life was scary. It is not by chance that I am here today. If I had given up and not put myself into action, I would likely be dead, a prostitute, a drug addict, or all of the above in reverse order. I needed to address my fears and put myself into action despite my trepidation. The power of the pause is in breathing long enough to listen, reveal, and heal.

As a speaking coach, I have observed how speakers employ the pause. Skilled speakers use the pause strategically to deliver a powerful talk. Professional speakers know the secret: the longer the pause, the greater the effect. A measured pause between speaking increases tension, underlines a point, enhances a joke, or wraps up a segment. Inexperienced speakers race through the pause and fail to anchor in their content. They have material to deliver, and they are going to get to it. I teach the power of the pause differently. Like the inexperienced speaker, many of us have a similar problem in our lives. We race over the moments that have the most significant impact on our lives and healing. Better to take a moment and pause.

Give yourself time to see if you are triggered so you can reflect and understand why. Then you can figure out how to neutralize the emotion. Pausing is for slowing down to notice what you are noticing. I love this saying so much I will make it our next rewiring process.

Notice What You Are Noticing: This practice has been instrumental in my growth because it helped me notice the world and how I react to it. The key idea is "how I react." I lived a reactive life and needed to learn how to respond more consciously to my environment, people, and situations.

Please pay attention to *notice what you are noticing in* your surroundings; it is vital to your healing. A great way to document your observations is to narrow down your significant triggers. You will want to keep a daily journal of your emotions. You can keep it simple to identify people, places, and things that elicit an emotion from you. You can then determine the actual event that ingrained the trigger.

Start by writing about the feeling and recording the first time you felt that feeling. It might look like this: a bill comes in and you start to freak out about money. You start on a rampage of panic and list all the bills you have and what is in your bank accounts. Then, you remember the power of the pause. You stop and reflect on the first time you felt this feeling. The memory of you in the hallway listening to your parents argue about money comes to you. They are freaking out about the finances. This awareness is powerful: you have just discovered you have an inherited money program from your parents' argument all those years ago.

Letting Go: Letting go is essential to releasing your victimhood. Until it is clear to you that you are running a victim program, you may hold tight to the feelings of bitterness and resentment from past hurts. This resistance will color your everyday life experiences and cause you to misinterpret well-meaning kindness and acts from others negatively.

Letting go is about your response to the pain or hurt inflicted on you. In the pause, you begin to transform the emotion into compassion, empathy, and understanding for the other. Find the inner strength to move beyond your pain to find inner peace and freedom.

Understand, you will have many moments when old feelings will arise. When this happens, don't analyze the hell out of them or let them trigger and overwhelm you into victimhood. Instead, give yourself permission to sit with them for a specific amount of time and reflect on what they mean to you. Acknowledge them, and make your way through them.

Build Self-Confidence: Healing your way out of the rubble of abuse can leave you feeling flawed, less than, and broken. You can address that work by building your self-confidence, which is not a natural characteristic; you learn, reinforce, and increase it in yourself.

*   *   *

As we work through the chapters, you will find your external actions reflect your empowered internal state. You will never again underestimate your power, nor undermine it. You will speak up, stand up, and play full out. I live by this motto, and my actions are nothing shy of powerful. I was not always like this. If someone looked at me wrong, I was a mess. I apologized for being alive. Today, I make no apologies for who I am and how I live in the true missing peace.

Ask yourself, what if instead of being victim to your life, you dedicated yourself to owning up to your shortcomings, failures, disappointments, and excuses, and committed to willingly forging ahead? What if your only option is to move forward through the obstacles life has thrown your way? What if you were willing to face the incredible fear of disappointment, shame, and humiliation? What if you let go of the grudge, heartache, and pain? Are you willing to dig deeper and push yourself further?

We are going to jump into more techniques to reprogram your subconscious mind which will help you believe in yourself because your confidence will no longer be challenged by judgment, others, fear, doubt, and your past. We will retrain and rewire your brain to be more resilient and aligned with your true desires, dreams, and life goals.

CHAPTER 8

Evolve Your Mind

Reader beware! From this point forward, you will enter into a realm of expansion and evolution. You will become increasingly unrecognizable. People will wonder what you have done to yourself. Some will not even know how to relate to you because you will reveal the missing piece of your life's puzzle.

This chapter is the beginning of the big reveal to *OR* living. Revealing the missing peace and piece will allow you to grow from victim to surviv*OR*, to a thriver, and finally to a fulfilled, empowered person. I made my commitment to write this book in the late '80s. I wanted to stop the cycle of abuse and further support others in shortcutting the healing process to make permanent changes. There is nothing you cannot overcome and transform. You will accomplish your most remarkable healing from the inside out.

We are going to dive deep into the mind to look at your conditioning, programming, training, and wiring, including your strengths and weaknesses. You will learn the art and science behind who you are and who you will be. You will be astonished at the power of your mind; it can easily change your impression of the past.

The Wiring in Your Mind

Let's begin by looking at the wiring in your mind. It is one of your most powerful tools, the element of yourself that enables your awareness of the world, your experiences, your thoughts, and your feelings. Your mind is the faculty of your consciousness and thought.

I will dip into the science of the mind and give you a basic understanding of how we are who we are.

As we discussed in Chapter 3, we have a conscious and subconscious mind. The conscious mind is your awareness at the present moment. In addition to being aware of what is going on outside, you have some mental activity happening inside. You are aware, for example, of the chair you are sitting on, what you see and hear, and your breath.

The subconscious mind (SCM, also called the automatic mind) consists of stored information from your entire life and is continuously operating. You sleep; it doesn't. An event occurs and the SCM automatically brings forth any and all situations and feelings related to this event. In other words, it triggers all of the related emotions. A trigger is automatic and embedded in your mind by a thought or feeling, tripped without warning.

Let's look at it this way: your mind is like a computer. What sits on your desktop is like your conscious mind. What gets stored on your computer–your contacts, calendar, programs, spreadsheets, etc.–is like your subconscious mind.

To illustrate, the following kind of experience might ring a bell for some of you. Your seventeen-year-old is out for the evening and has an 11:30 pm curfew. You look at the clock and it is 11:45 pm. He is not home yet. That's okay; he's only a few minutes late, so no big deal. The next time you look, it is midnight, and now you are beginning to get annoyed. When it is 12:15 am, you start getting downright angry. You start to think of what you will do and say the minute he walks in the door. Yet, now it is 12:30 am, and you begin to recall every news report, TV show, movie, and accident you have heard about related to teens. Now, you are envisioning your precious kid in the ditch somewhere, fighting for his or her life. You begin to have a shortness of breath; sweat starts to bead, and you feel a full-on panic attack coming.

Here's what's happening behind the scenes. Your SCM is unable to distinguish fact from fiction. The SCM gets input from the senses and the conscious mind. Thoughts run through your mind continuously, both good and bad. The SCM takes the info and ideas coming in, then it searches for any evidence from the past, present, and other sources to provide a match to any input. As you defend your mood, your SCM is busy providing you with evidence about your bad hair day and the kids being late, all of which have traditionally caused you to be cranky and eventually fearful. As a result, you become cranky and eventually fearful, which is how you feel now.

Let me give you another example of how the SCM works. If I were to say to you, "Lemon, lemon candy, sucking on a lemon," your mouth would start to water. The SCM automatically recalls when you sucked on a lemon or anything that made your mouth pucker. When the SCM provides us the information or memories, we consciously label those thoughts as real.

With sexual abuse, a message that might be hard-wired is that sex is dirty. Therefore, every time you think about, pursue, or engage in sex, you might feel dirty or ashamed. The trigger is thoughts of sex, and the related response is the massive amounts of stored data in your SCM.

I worked on my sex programming for decades and found I was getting better and better around the meaning of sex and the self-judgment. I had NO idea there was a stone left unturned. My ex and I entered into therapy to attempt to re-ignite a fire in our relationship. My desire was for more communication, intimacy, connection, and growth with more limits on politics, news, and sports. During one of our therapy sessions, the therapist asked if either of us masturbated. Sure! Who doesn't? Not everyone, it turns out.

My ex was furious! She responded with a very bold and harsh statement: "You may as well have an affair on me!" The instant she said that my entire system shut down. I felt shame, guilt, and humiliation. For me, sex was to be secretive and covert, alone or with another, remember? What had I done? I thought I was doing us a favor by taking care of myself to avoid any affairs. I just confessed my sexual activity and was shot down. It was an eye-opening trigger I was unaware I had running.

As we discussed in Chapter 5, who you are and how you live is based on the past story. Spoiler alert: these are lies, all lies. We have ongoing programs running in the background. Remember good ole Pavlov's Dog[4]? You live according to outdated beliefs, stories, and patterns, automatically responding to the signal of triggers on autopilot. Your SCM accesses patterns and programs from your past, and this data supports your comfort zone, keeping you safe. How do you discover these patterns that have become bad habits and rewire new information and beliefs into your SCM? Think of it as a full-time job with a consistent awareness of what you are thinking, feeling, doing, and noticing.

While new good habits help you live a regular life, you will forever live in a *Groundhog Day* style of existence if you don't break the bad habits with rewiring. Remember, neurons that fire together, wire together. We are going to fire up some new thinking and being.

---

[4] Pavlov, Ivan. 1849-1936, Nobel Prize in Physiology or Medicine (1904)

Imagine life is like a pole vault bar that is higher than twenty feet tall. Now, if you measured everything according to this bar, including your desires, big ideas, or dreams, you will automatically and unconsciously reject anything above the bar that you think is more than you can attain or that you deserve. To make a change, it will take time and dedication for you to rewire your subconscious mind to accept there is life beyond the twenty-foot limit.

The good news is you will be shocked at the progress you make in a short time when you do the work. To achieve success, you must have a program or wiring aligned with your desired outcome. You can't think of success and failure at the same time. With opposing thoughts, the mind can't rationalize or think through what you intend. Whatever you believe, the SCM will bring about that result. In other words, the SCM is a magnet to your dominant belief and automatic wiring.

The work is to begin to input new and improved stories and beliefs into the subconscious mind. You don't have to *get rid of anything*; you withdraw your attention from the old.

Have you ever gone to a baseball game? Between innings, the crew drags the field to wipe out the past play. Similarly, you are working to clean the ground of your past. Or better yet, think of the old programs you have as a work of art on an Etch A Sketch. You are going to shake it up and rid your mind of the past you.

The process of taking your limiting stories and beliefs and turning them into the desired outcome is very simple and straightforward–but it's not always easy. Your abuse sets you up to believe things that aren't true. Even though most of what you think and believe about yourself is inaccurate and distorted, the program continues to run. Good news! You can transform your beliefs into powerful positive results.

Let's look at how you can go from an inherited or ingrained belief about yourself to knowing the truth. I want to walk you through the following three steps:

1. realize
2. release and re-pattern, and
3. align

Realize

The first step is to find out what is true about you, despite what others have said or done. When you identify the story you tell about yourself, you will transform everything in your life.

For example, in the past, I told the world that God forgot me. I concluded very early in life that God had forgotten me because no God would allow this form of abuse to happen to anyone, nor would a good God take away my mother. That story resulted in feelings of abandonment and aloneness, and it was a painful story to carry around. My God story was paralyzing at times. I had developed a story and needed to put this belief into perspective, or I was never going to be fulfilled, not to mention successful.

What is your "God forgot me" story?

Make a list of the statements you tell about yourself:

- Do you say you are fat?
- Do you believe you are never going to amount to anything?
- What excuses do you make?
- What is your go-to statement about yourself?

Everyone has a story about themselves, good or bad. Identify what stories you tell about yourself.

Here are a few short story examples:

- "I'm not smart enough."
- "I have no degree."
- "I'm unlovable."
- "I am an addict."
- "I'm too old, too young."
- "I'm too tall, too skinny, too fat."
- "I'm too (something)!"

Many people also make very definitive statements about themselves, their life, or current conditions. Remember, the SCM is a magnet to your dominant belief or most powerful story you tell. If you believe you can't get the promotion because you are too old, you won't get it. If you want to lose that last five pounds and you believe you can't lose weight no matter what, guess what? Those darn five pounds will not go away (trust me, I know). Henry Ford said, "Whether you think you can or think you can't, you are right."

Recognize your story by listening to what you say and what you think. Keep your list handy and add to it. You will discover and realize more stories that bubble up as you continue to experience more growth and success. Track the current ones you tell over and over again.

Release and Rewire

A story or statement you think or tell about yourself must be positive or empowering. If it is not, this is a story you need to release. The goal is to create a new you and begin to drag the past like that baseball field. You are not what they said about you. You are not what happened to you. The opportunity for growth comes when you can stop rehearsing the story over and over again.

Keep in mind this doesn't happen overnight. You have been running around for years telling and believing these things about yourself. The stories feel real. I swore that God did forget me. Until I did the work it was so real, and I could show evidence when things didn't work out for me. Transforming what feels like a fact into a new truth requires you to think differently, create a new story, and rewire your mind, creating a new you.

Your new story is far greater than any facts you believed or even facts you see every day. Facts can change; the truth is constant. And you are creating a new reality. The process of re-wiring takes discipline and your attention.

When I get into my car, I turn on the radio. I have the control to turn up the volume or turn it down. This choice is the same as with your thinking and storytelling. You will not try to get rid of the old thinking or story; you will turn up the new volume. The wiring initially created pathways by repetition and trauma. The rewiring is the same process. You will override the old circuits with new and improved lines.

Another example of the need for rewiring happened in our historic 1920 home in downtown Phoenix. When we were remodeling our kitchen, we discovered the drain lines were crumbling. Not just a little, mind you. The entire line was disintegrating from the house to the curb. The plumber didn't work to remove all the lines, however; he laid new ones. The old pipes will eventually corrode as will your old programs.

Keep in mind, the words you speak are just the tip of the iceberg. The needle mover for your rewiring, in either direction, are the emotions behind your words. We say many words and phrases that have the power to make or break our success.

Let's look at a few:

Should: This is a biggie! You have heard of the saying, don't *should* on yourself, or others for that matter. *Should* is loaded with doubt and disappointment, intended to motivate you or keep you in check, and unleashes a myriad of feelings, including frustration, guilt, pressure, stress, and regret. *Should* is a powerful word that has the potential of creating an SCM mine-field, creating expectations that set you up for failure; it is a form of self-sabotage.

My father set up my *shoulds* my entire life. My father expected my sister and me to run the whole household. He often traveled, and upon his arrival home, we were to have a full refrigerator, cleaned and folded laundry, a tidy house, completed errands, and dinner on the table. On the weekends, we had many chores to do.

I remember one hot summer day. I had moved over twenty-five-wheelbarrows full of large gravel. Now, I need a little lovin' here: I was fifteen years old, standing all of 5'4" weighing in at ninety-eight pounds soaking wet. I was exhausted. So, I took a load off and flopped onto the couch. I sat for all of three minutes and my father walked in and said, "It must be nice to have the luxury of being so lazy. Some of us have work to do, and it isn't going to do itself."

What was my inner response, as I quickly got up and went back to the gravel pit? *I should have been more dedicated. I should have lived up to his expectations. I should be more like him.* Really, I *should* have said, "You know what you can do with your gravel?" Instead, what did I do? I inherited the use of *should* to motivate me.

You have inherited *should* into your vocabulary. Let's ditch it now! Start by catching yourself every time that word comes out of your mouth or into your mind. Stop beating yourself up over what you think you should or shouldn't do. You now know these expectations are not your own. Others instilled them: your parents, boss, society, the Joneses, and now you.

It is a tough habit to break and goes back to our concept of *notice what you are noticing*. Pay attention, as healing is not for the faint of heart or the lazy. When you find yourself using the word, simply pause for a moment and take notice of it. You can then say to yourself or out loud: "Let me reframe that, 'What I would love to do is _____.'" And then, go one step further and list out the benefits of your desired action.

I AM: Using I AM is a way to claim or take ownership over a state of being, action, or trait. You can use the I AM statement for or against yourself. Many unconsciously use the I AM statement negatively, such as:

- I am never able to sleep
- I am stupid
- I am always late
- I am dying to get out of here

- I am sick and tired
- I am stuck
- I am never going to get ahead

All of these statements claim an adverse effect or result. No one desires negativity; however, you are claiming whatever follows it each time you say I AM. What you claim is yours whether you realize you are claiming it or not!

Now, what if you start writing I AM positive statements on sticky notes and posting them throughout your surroundings? It's essential to include the words and also feel the emotions behind the words. For example, walk naked into your bathroom and post on the mirror a sticky note that reads, "I AM SKINNY." You take a glance and see that your love handles have seemingly grown as has your Buddha belly. You may think, "Skinny? Are you kidding me? Dang it!" The dominant belief you have in this case is "I AM fat or chubby." Emotions will supersede any I AM statement.

For years, my go-to worry was I AM broke. Realistically, I have never, nor will I ever be broke. Why? My dominant belief, which is stronger than my go-to worry, is I AM always taken care of, and everything works out for me. Deep down, I know I will always create a flow of wealth coming to me. At night, I go to bed affirming: "Money and wealth beyond measure come to me, easily, effortlessly, immediately, and consistently. I AM rich." I practiced truly embracing the feeling of this statement over and over again until it feels familiar. So, now I am not shocked when wealth appears *out of the blue*. I simply think, well of course. (Oh, by the way, "the blue" in the expression "out of the blue" is your mind made manifest.) Remember earlier, when I expressed my thoughts around "I AM a survivor"? I continue to encourage you to do so, too. I hope this helps you further understand that you are more than your past.

I Can't: While you may not say it out loud, you may think it far too many times. By saying *"I can't,"* even if it's only in your thoughts, you set yourself up for failure because it means you give up. Catch yourself when you say it. Maybe what you mean is, "I won't" or "I don't know how to *yet*," and you are not stating whether you are able or not able to do it. I will share the best comeback line of all time. When you catch yourself saying, "I can't," you respond to yourself, "And what if I could?"

I Have a Problem: You can see a problem as a situation preventing something from being achieved. You hear people say all the time, "I have a problem." I find myself immediately taking a deep breath when someone makes that comment, taking ownership, and claiming it as their own.

When you call something a problem, you create a feeling of stress because you have a lot of work to devise a solution. And stress creates foggy or lackluster thinking that blocks your creativity and inhibits your ability to find a solution quickly. I like to say, "I have an opportunity."

Obstacles are a chance to grow and overcome. The word "opportunity" focuses on a set of circumstances that open up the possibility of doing something. Substitute the word "problem" with "opportunity" and see how well it goes.

Just: This word is a tough one. You can *just* do it, or it can be a qualifier. We often use it to minimize ourselves, our possessions, and our accomplishments. When asked what you do, do you say things like, "I'm *just* a stay at home mom," or "I'm *just* starting my business," or "I'm *just* a project manager," all sure-fire ways to devalue yourself and deflect any risk of them finding out, you aren't all that great. Wait, you are great! Never *just* yourself.

The other form of *just* is to tell you or someone else to *just* do it. In the world, we think it is effortless to *just*. *Just* make the sales calls, *just* get the degree, *just* date the person, *just* tell the person, *just* ask for what you need, *just* lose the weight, or *just* stop telling me to *just*. If you knew how to *just,* you would. The word *just* is loaded with a ton of resources, knowledge, and steps to take. In the absence of having the right support, information, and direction, *just* can be paralyzing. I know! One division of my coaching work is business coaching. Entrepreneurs, small business owners, and corporations hire me to help them *just*. I provide them every step necessary for success, from messaging to sales conversations. Why? Because if they *just* did it themselves, their businesses would still be in the hopes and dreams pile.

Try: Either you are going to do it or not. It's like being pregnant. You can't be sorta pregnant; you either are, or you are not. There's an instructive scene in the *Star Wars* movie, *The Empire Strikes Back.* Yoda is instructing Luke Skywalker on how to use the Force. He asks Luke to retrieve his disabled spaceship from a bog where it has sunk, using only his mind. Luke, of course, thinks this is impossible. Sure, he has been able to move stones around this way, but a spaceship? That's completely different. Or is it?

Yoda patiently explains that it is only different *in his mind.* Luke reluctantly agrees to "give it a try." Yoda famously says, "No! Try not! Do. Or do not. There is no try."

Trying requires no effort or commitment. Using the word *try* is self-defeating, as it indicates a lack of accomplishment. Compare the difference between "Try and stand up. Just try"– you would feel defeated from the start–and "Do your best to stand up." You would follow through and accomplish the task. Eliminate *try* from your vocabulary by substituting the phrase, "do your best." And then decide either to do it or not.

Align the Story

The third step to defining your truth is to rewire your new story in your mind. Transformation requires thinking in a way that is in alignment with the habits and behaviors you want to create.

Be aware, as you begin to feel good or sense you are on a new path, there will be an overwhelming pull from the past, also known as your old wiring, in your mind. You may not realize that you have a set habit or defined level of your success (think of the pole vault bar), which determines how good your life can be.

Some call it the glass ceiling, an unacknowledged barrier to your success and accomplishments. Gay Hendricks says it best in his book, *The Big Leap*, where he describes this as the "Upper Limit Problem." Practically all of us face an upper limit problem: parts of us are programmed to stay safe, not to shine, or to stand out in the crowd. As a result, we limit our success, wealth, health, and happiness in fear of the consequences. We hold ourselves back because we have a core set of beliefs that we will fail, we will be alone, or we are not enough.

However, this scenario doesn't have to be the case. You can align with a more empowering story and create a new upper limit that diminishes the power of the old fears, shifts the focus of your creativity, and drives you to your unique gift. Aligning with your new upper limit opens up to more abundant thoughts and requires you to expand your *awareness of what is possible*.

[5]Nelson Mandela said, "It always seems impossible until it's done." The old self wants to settle into the status quo. You may believe, "It is what it is." You want to get in the habit of using the phrase, "What if?" Challenge your old thinking by triggering curiosity as curiosity gets the imagination going, and you become aware of more possibilities.

---

5 Nelson Mandela. AZQuotes.com, WIND AND FLY LTD, 2018. http://azquotes.com/quote/185315 accessed 2017.

Stop and ask yourself right now, "What if?" and fill in the blank. What if the love of my life dropped out of the blue? What if I could feel adventurous and proud of my sexy curiosity? What if I could drop twenty pounds?

When you ask "what if" questions, your mind will begin to create a picture of that "what if," and you will be open to imagining. If I were to say the word "Hawaii," for example, your mind will see a beach, crystal-clear water, a lounge chair, and a little drink with an umbrella. If I were to say "think about your car, kitchen, or pet," your mind will visually recall each item or person. Even better, if I were to say, DO NOT picture the Statue of Liberty or do not see Lady Liberty standing tall in the harbor, it backfires. You cannot help but create a visual of the Statue of Liberty! This process of imagining is how you take preference and transform it into results. You will begin to imagine, vividly, what it would look like to have, be, or do what you prefer.

Imagination is the quickest way to create something in your life, good or bad. In 1989, my dear friend and speaking coach, Glenna Salsbury, taught me a potent formula:

$$\text{Vividness} \times \text{Imagination} = \text{Reality}$$

I've adapted and enhanced her formula to read:

$$\text{Vividness} \times \text{Imagination} \times \textbf{Emotion} = \text{Reality}^2 \text{ (squared)}$$

You square your results by adding emotion to the formula. By feeling the results that you want to create, you supercharge the equation. It's essential to understand it is all about the feelings related to what you desire, rather than what it is. Let me explain. Many people *want* because they don't *have*, and the mind doesn't understand the difference between "don't want" and "want." The mind only responds to emotion.

I love asking, "What if?" because it puts an immediate stop to any doubtful thinking and allows me to open to what is possible. The question frustrates the mind's status quo (what we call the comfort zone) because anything is possible when you accept it as your new truth. Seeing what is possible will create new ideas, images, resources, and a flow of understanding that opens us up to choices and decisions we can put into action.

I have dedicated my entire life to revealing the missing peace, power, and success. I have always gotten results from any career I have chosen. I have never been broke financially. Yet, despite all my "success," there was still something missing. Unknowingly, my drive was an effort to fill the void my abuse left in me. I had no idea. I thought I was just a driven person and took pride in that.

You may be a driven person in one area or all areas of your life. You may be going after that promotion, relationship, status, image, or money. You may not know you are basing your quest on a false desire that turns into a destructive drive. Having the drive to succeed is fine if it is for the right reasons. I would venture to guess most survivors are doing everything in their power to fill the void. After extensive research and conversations, I have found this to be true amongst the women and men I spoke to concerning their drive.

If you take anything away from this book, please make it be the fact you do not need to fill any void. When I refer to the void, I am referring to a feeling that something is missing. You have a great life–BUT. The BUT is that feeling of needing more or a lack of dissatisfaction. The void will be demonstrated in your life uniquely.

My void has been a desperate need for security. You may feel a sense of longing for love or adventure. Others may find it expressed as self-sabotage or self-destruction, depression, isolation, emotional emptiness, no sense of purpose, no direction, overly busy, or an uninteresting life. The void is due to your abuse. It is a sense of loss or unfulfilled internal desires due to fear, doubt, conditioning, shame, and guilt. It is a yearning for love and a trusting connection.

In short, the void leaves you with a variety of restless feelings:

- You want to be left alone
- You feel life is meaningless
- You are not attracted to anyone
- Absence of happiness
- You feel like you have to fill your void, typically through addiction to alcohol and drugs
- You are always bored
- Fear of being left alone
- Feeling empty/hollow inside
- The absence of true happiness or fulfillment
- Addictive behavior (to escape the emptiness)
- Emotional numbness\
- Inability to slow down/workaholism (as a form of escape)
- Chronic boredom

Let's explore what is behind this void by looking at a significant finding based on a 2019 study by Angi Jacobs-Kayam and Rachel Lev-Wiesel, *In Limbo: Time Perspective and Memory Deficit Among Female Survivors of Sexual Abuse.*

The study showed survivors related to a feeling of missing out on pivotal life experiences and periods following the abuse. They expressed various feelings from living on the sidelines and unable to account for their experiences while being aware of time passing. This lack of knowledge regarding one's experiences left survivors struggling to trust themselves and learn from their past. This void or sense that something is missing results in an emptiness that triggers the need to fill the void. A person in this state of void finds themselves in crap relationships, unfulfilling careers, pleasing others, sacrificing desires, inadequate intimacy, damaging encounters, and overeating or undereating.

The study states that child sexual abuse survivors frequently described their lives as a state of limbo, with central parts of their selves a mystery, adrift in space and time without an anchor, devoid of positive memories of the past before the abuse. The abuse obliterated their previous identity. Sexual abuse is a life experience that leaves a residue on survivors' psyches. The experience cannot be erased or forgotten at will and survivors find their way, often subconsciously, to deal with the harmful effect abuse has on them by separating themselves from it in a manner that allows them to function.

As a survivor, you are highly skilled at compartmentalizing: you put feelings and events in their proper place, resulting in burying or expressing. For example, my abuse left me feeling epically flawed. I locked that compartment behind multiple barriers deep in a safe, with no lock. I was not going to allow anyone to find out there was something wrong with me. So, to cover up my flaws, I overachieved. I outpaced anyone in my career and life. The outer results showed there was nothing wrong with me, while the inside was a mess. The harder I drove for glory, the bigger the mess got. I was in an endless race to never allow my past to catch up with me. I thought I could fill the void and bury the past. No such luck!

As a result of being abused, you have developed a sense of dread. There is an anticipation of the next inevitable other-shoe-dropping event coming your way, which is much like the conditioned anticipation of the subsequent encounter with the abuser. Thus you end up in a perpetual cycle of dread in your adult life. It is a conditioned response. You never get too excited for fear there will be a great disappointment.

The cycle of anticipation results in an internal drive to prevent the next roadblock in your life, which is exhausting. I know it, I lived it! Do you want to know the worst part? It is grueling work to create success differently. I have created three multi-million-dollar businesses and built them out of pure fear, drive, and adrenaline. There was a fear in me and a void to fill, a recipe for disaster, yet it worked for me. I kept moving, so I didn't have to experience the fear or deal with the truth behind my need for more. You may not even realize there is a part of you seeking fulfillment and success.

Denise spent years thinking everything was fine, and life just happened. Her job was to handle everything that came her way when it did. While she recognized things would happen just as she thought they would, Denise had yet to realize she was drawing these experiences to herself. She was asleep and never had any idea her mind was as powerful as she now knows it to be.

*   *   *

When you want to do anything in your life, you must form an image. The trick is to keep the old habits from overpowering the new vision, as this is the key to your creation of everything. Now, remember, I *did* say it was simple, but you should know it's not easy. When you overcome a past program, you will have to deal with it again. Our programs and habits are always there, lurking in the background, waiting to be triggered. They are not waiting to sabotage us; they are there to protect us. As we grow in our healing, we will need (and want) to do things outside of our comfort zone. That is where our programs sit in wait and then, bam! They show up. The key is to practice the steps of transformation continually.

When we commit to rewiring our minds, we make it happen. As they say, go big or go home. Since we are on a *Star Wars* roll, I will again reference Yoda, who encourages Luke to unlearn what he has learned. I encourage you to unlearn what you know. Drag the field of your mind or shake up the Etch A Sketch and let's do our best to rock all you desire.

These are the basics of releasing and rewiring. I want you to begin by being honest with yourself as you go under a microscope. It is the only way to bring to your awareness of the many programs running your life. You are at the hands of your old programs, and likely don't know what the heck those are. Please keep working on realizing and releasing the habits and patterns of your life. If you attempt to do this next step and bypass the real work, it will fail. You SHOULD (just kidding) because then you GET to free yourself from the past.

CHAPTER 9

Achieve a New Reality

What if you had all the power within you to create a new life? What if everything you learned about hereditary traits, genetics, and DNA was wrong? What if you could change the course of your life using the power of your thoughts? Would you do it? Of course, you would!

You are not victim to your gene pool, only to your thoughts. Whether you choose Alcoholics Anonymous (AA), Narcotics Anonymous (NA), Overeaters Anonymous (OA), Gamblers Anonymous (GA), or any other A, the first step in sobriety is to admit you are powerless over alcohol/drugs/sex/chemicals. Since you are reading this book, you are also willing to acknowledge that your life is unmanageable, inside, outside, or both.

The funny thing is, no one looking from the outside would have ever described my life as being unmanageable. There was not one day in my life that my outside world would ever appear to be anything other than extraordinary. From the time I entered school, I was the smiling, helpful teacher's pet. The Academy should have given me an Oscar for my award-winning performance as a model child from a loving family. As I was moving through my healing, I did something interesting. I went back and interviewed my teachers and coaches. I asked them what they thought of me or how they perceived my life to be.

All of them said I seemed to be extremely happy and well-adjusted to my mother's death. Many credited this to my family of origin. They had the impression my family was attentive and loving for me to be such a fantastic kid. My physical education teacher and basketball coach stated that sometimes I seemed withdrawn a bit, but had a remarkable ability to bounce back.

I listened with shock and dismay. I could not imagine how anyone missed the signs. To me, I felt like I had "I am being abused" on my forehead. I had convinced myself that everyone could tell, and yet no one could. After each conversation, I asked if I could share my experience with them and educate them about abuse. They were all open, and then utterly stunned, at my reveal.

My life was so unbelievably unmanageable on the inside, yet no one knew it, only me. Likewise, only you can determine your unmanageability level. Meanwhile, you can still function. It might be that you have a sense of something missing or a feeling of carrying a dirty little secret. There are varying degrees of unmanageability and it may be a desire for so much more. Either way, you are here to be, do, and have more. And that is what we are going to address now.

Commit to a New Way of Being You

In an earlier chapter, I provided essential information about the SCM, the subconscious mind, so you understand how you think and feel is what creates your reality. Life is a mirror of your thinking, based mostly on the past. The SCM runs us with information we have inherited, learned, and acquired, and stores events in our lives: abuse, neglect, bullying, trauma, divorce, rejection, failure, and relocation, including what you don't remember.

The data stored goes into a *file* of similar data in your SCM. The more you access the file, the more data is loaded. It is similar to your search history on the internet. When you search the web, you store cookies or cache, a widely used method for storing information later accessed much more quickly. In the SCM, data is also immediately retrievable at all times.

Our work together is going to be focused on creating a new mind resulting in a new you. My ask of you is that you are open and willing to commit to a new way of being you. For several decades, I have been studying the greats in the world of personal development and expansion. My studies range from brain science and spiritual principles to quantum physics. My conclusion: they are all the same. And what they share is this: the way you think and feel creates your reality. Whether you ask your high power to bring it forth or you consciously use the power of your mind, all paths lead to expansion of you.

The content of this chapter will tempt you to turn and run or maybe throw up your hands and give up. When I began this work, I felt like I was not making any progress at all.

The process of rewiring and creating a new life takes patience, patience, and yes, more patience. If I can do it, as one of the most impatient people on the planet, you can do it. Stay committed and stay the course. I will guide you through a new way of thinking and being.

Getting started requires you to embrace the fact that your thoughts have consequences. You will need to understand and accept that the statement "I am who I am" will no longer work for you. You can and will transform the way you are today. You are not your past nor are you a victim of past thinking. You need to own that every thought you have produces a real thing or event. The inside world of thought will produce tangible effects in your life. It's the principle of cause and effect. You have an idea (the cause), and this thought makes a result (the effect).

Currently, I am willing to guess you wake each day to a routine. You get up, brush your teeth, shower, shave, and shine. You drive the same routes and seek consistency in your life. As a survivor, the known is far safer than surprises.

The Definition of Insanity

You have likely heard the quote: "The definition of insanity is doing the same thing over and over again and expecting different results." If we think the same way and act the same way every day, how can we get different results? We don't mean to be insane; we think how we always do, based upon what we know.

When you know that cells absorb the repetition of the same thought patterns, why do you insist on doing it? Addiction! You are addicted to sameness or the known.

If you experienced chaos while growing up, you have a thought pattern that is a magnet to chaos. If you grew up poor and lacking the basic needs of life, you have a thought pattern that is a magnet to either being broke or a terrible fear of being broke. If you grew up in abuse, you have a thought pattern that is a magnet to abuse. Your mind develops the same thought patterns that change you at a cellular level: your body and mind become one.

The basic premise of this work is to understand and observe the power of your mind. You get to consciously decide what you will think and break the cycle of habits, triggers, and beliefs that no longer serve you. Until you accept you are the reason (also known as the co-creator) for everything in your life, you will continue to be a victim to your circumstances.

Create with Intentional Thoughts

Decide to create with intentional thoughts rather than by default. You will take your mind as you know it and perform a complete makeover, which will require admitting and knowing what is real and authentic. If you can predict and prepare for your outcomes, as we did in the earlier chapter about recognizing signs and symptoms, triggers, and behaviors, it allows you to be safe and sound. When you manage your risk and the element of surprise, you no longer have to live a life solely based on your past. You get to take control.

For example, I met a woman in the San Diego airport one day. I was coming off of the plane as she was waiting to board. We were in the smaller terminal where the jetway was narrow and tight. She was a very tall model traveling for a photo session, although she didn't look so beautiful at this moment. She was in a full-blown panic attack. When I stopped and asked her if I could support her, she could barely talk. Trembling, she stuttered, "I'm NOT going to be able to get on the plane!" Fear was raging through her body and mind.

This woman didn't say to her body, "It is time to freak the heck out because we hate flying, and it is a tiny plane." She had a thought which triggered fear, and her body went on autopilot, pun intended. She didn't have to tell her body to sweat, shake, feel light-headed, or throw up. Her body took control without any direction.

However, she was in luck as I had recently received my training about interrupting the pattern of thought. Quickly taking action, I told the model, "I have a great technique that will eliminate this panic attack and any others in the future."

I got her attention with my powerful technique (which I had just made up, by the way; it was an ethical endorsement of my new-found skill). I told her that if she took her index finger and touched the tip of every finger on her other hand five times around, she would begin to calm down. I stood there with her, as we both did the technique. After about the third time around, her breathing calmed, and she started to feel better. She turned and gave me the biggest hug of gratitude. I waited until she stepped onto the plane with a big smile and wave for me.

Your mind has no idea if something is made up on the fly or came from a New York University scientific study. Frankly, your mind doesn't care. But you do. You base your perception of your environment, situations, or people on past experiences. You have assigned meaning to everything.

Conditioning your mind is easy. You think a thought enough times, it becomes a part of your cellular make up. Your body will continuously give you a stream of reliable information about your experiences in the form of sensation. Remember, your SCM is a database of you at the deepest level, including all your adventures.

Understanding Your Body Sensations

The relationship between your body and mind is vital to your healing and transformation. To create a permanent change, you must reprogram your mind to recondition your body, which requires you to think greater than your environment and the external stimulus. You will begin to respond to life rather than react to it. This process is a complete house cleaning of those experiences that have become part of your cellular makeup.

Think of your healing like the city of Rome. Like Europe's other ancient cities, Rome perches on one vast archeological site. The modern city sits on top of the residue of earlier ones, stretching back almost three millennia. As each city took form, the existing structures collapsed or filled in with dirt to form the buildings' foundation of the next stage of the city's evolution. Buildings rested on other constructions, and roofs became foundations. Each layer was successively covered up, gradually morphing into modern Rome's elaborate archeological layer cake.

"Rome wasn't built in a day," nor will you be. Transforming your old patterns of thinking and retraining your body to respond differently is a process that takes time and patience.

Thoughts, Emotions, and Energy

How do you begin? To start, come from a place of curiosity. Consider that multiple generations of parents created your programming. The inherited reactions and patterns passed down through endless generations do not work in your life today. Your mission is to question every idea or reaction that is not your own.

For example, while I have never been financially broke, my mind forever loves to remind me of my program around money. Usually when I am mountain biking, I hear a little voice in my head, encouraging me to get back to work or we might lose everything. While I have never lost anything, let alone everything, my mother did. My grandfather lost the farm due to his alcoholism. I inherited my mother and father's fear of losing it all. This fear has been a very significant hurdle for me to overcome, requiring endless days of reprogramming.

If you go back to the equation, *Vividness x Imagination x **Emotion** = Reality²*, you will be reminded that the emotion is the power booster. The more intensely you feel about a person, place, or thing, the more magnified the attraction. For your work and healing, I would ask you to think of your mind and body as an electrically charged system. Since our thoughts carry an energy field and cause the cells to react, it is safe to say we are all energetic beings.

If we look at this from the standpoint of God, we can look at it the same way. Follow my thinking here: God has no beginning and no end, as does energy. Energy is all-pervasive, as is God. There is no place where the energy is absent, and no place where God is NOT. We can only feel; energy cannot be seen, nor can God. Both are invisible.

Scientists have faith in energy, and theists have faith in God. If you are a believer or a faith-filled God-loving person, then you talk to Him all the time. You are harnessing the power of God's grace, aka energy, in your life. You understand spiritual strength through prayer. This oneness with God is the secret of unlimited energy. Whether communicating with God or life, when you think a thought, you get a result. Think and feel into the thought, and you get a more outstanding result.

Following the Quantum Mechanics of the Law of Attraction, you attract into your life those things, circumstances, and conditions that correspond with the nature of your dominant, habitual thoughts and beliefs, both conscious and subconscious. Every area of your life, including your health, finances, and relationships, is influenced by this great universal law that "like attracts like." Eugene Fersen, in the *Science of Being*, referred to the Law of Attraction as "the Basic Law of the Universe."

What if you decided to tap into a new innovative idea and desire to be bright-eyed and bushy-tailed in the morning? You are modeling after someone who loves to wake up early and seize the day with joy and freedom. Your old state of being might be fearful, worried, contrary, defensive, act like a victim, or all of the above. Your new state of being is joyful and free.

Let's get rid of all programs that no longer serve us and tap into new endless potentials. And let's do it now, rather than when things get so bad you cannot focus. It seems to be human nature not to make the necessary changes until things get desperate. Most people wait until they are so uncomfortable that they can no longer go on as usual. You don't have to be most people. Do not wait for a crisis, diagnosis, trauma, loss, disease, or tragedy to decide to embrace change. As a survivOR, don't plan for a worst-case scenario; it's time to make changes that support your life.

Putting It in Action as a SurvivOR

Meanwhile, you can guarantee that life will continue to throw challenges your way. How do you react to a new crisis with your newly reprogrammed brain? Let me share an example.

As a result of my abuse, I had a fear program running most of my life. When I rented my first apartment, I was confident we had done our homework and determined this was a safe place to live. My apartment was in Wheaton, Illinois, which is known to be a mostly Christian town. When my partner and I moved in, this reputation gave us a very good feeling–until that hot summer night at 12:31 am.

While we were asleep in our waterbed (yes, a waterbed, I know), I heard a squeak. Sleepy, I attempted to focus my eyes on the doorway, a familiar action from my earlier abuse with many *shadowed doorway* memories. Immediately I held my breath when I saw the bedroom door slowly swing open and watched as a very tall man entered our room.

Terrified, my mind raced about how to survive the potential danger we faced. As I mentioned, we were in a waterbed. If you haven't been in one for a while or ever, you sink far into the bed. Thank goodness because the perpetrator could not figure out who was in bed. After what felt like a lifetime of contemplation by this man, he turned and left.

The result of this bedroom invasion was that my old program of fear and sexual abuse conditioning resurfaced. I became a victim again, and I felt vulnerable, unsafe, and anticipated more attacks. I would think about the incident over and over again, feeling the outrageous fear of the danger. I was right on track with filling in the equation *Vividness x Imagination x* **Emotion** *= Reality^2*. I had the vividness of the event as I could see it so clearly, invested in imagining the worst-case scenario, as well as what I should have done. I had an elevated emotion of fear and vulnerability. All of this equated to Reality^2.

My reality began showing up in awful ways all over the place. The first incident was in the movie theater when a man was having a field day pleasuring himself in the row behind me. The next was at the pool when a man exposed himself to a few of us. I realized my thoughts were attracting this reality after a few more instances. I did the work and addressed my fear program once again.

When your life seems to be a frustrating stream of the same adverse outcomes, be mindful of your thoughts, emotions, and energy. While you now understand the connection, it is easy to fall back into old patterns. For example, you may be thinking and feeling about how you would love to have a great new job. At the same time, however, you are thinking about everything wrong with the current one. You get an interview and land the job, only to find out it is the same job with a different company. Too often, this happens in the world of dating. How many of you have dated or married the same person over and over again? You think about what you don't want, which affects the electromagnetic field and draws to you the same darn person.

Trust All Will Unfold

In the book *Becoming Supernatural*, Dr. Joe Dispenza talks about "causing an effect." I love this principle. Instead of being a victim to the effect, we can cause it, which means we can intentionally determine our outcomes. Most everyone focuses on the HOW when the HOW is none of our business. We are not the ones to determine how we will affect the result; we can have faith.

I do my best every day to walk through life like a surprise party is ready to happen at any minute. I anticipate the unexpected. If I can predict the exact outcome, then it is something I have experienced or faced before, just a slightly different version. If it is a surprise and the effect is beyond what I imagined, then I have successfully partnered with the Infinite.

The most significant work you will have to do in creating your new state of being is to surrender. Trust all will unfold. Let go of how it *should* look and wait for the big surprise. As a surviv*OR*, this will prove to be the biggest hurdle to overcome.

The unknown is a terrifying place. It leaves many feeling out of control, and we want to control the outcome. While you base your new mode of creating on your thinking and feeling, reality and results are dependent and delayed. The field of possibility takes a bit longer to catch up to your desire. The physical evidence of desires (effect) becomes a reality after pushmi-pullyu (known as a *push-me-pull-you*). A pushmi-pullyu, according to My Dictionary, is a fictional animal with two heads at opposing ends of its body, and which readily faced contradictory thoughts and reactions.

As you move through your work in creating a new state of being, you will find your new thoughts will bring up doubt, and you will find you are at odds with each part of you internally. One part of you will have no doubt you can cause your desired effect and the other part of you will think not. You will be in constant conflict with yourself, going in opposite directions, one to the old, the other to the new. Trust me; the old has a solid foundation in your mind. It will take outstanding commitment and effort to outsmart the old.

Gratitude = Fastest Path to a New State of Being

The next step in establishing a new state of being is to practice gratitude. And it is hard. Being grateful before the results show up can be frustrating. We are going to be practicing gratitude for what is NOT yet in our reality. The cause is gratitude, the effect is the person, place, or thing.

The Bible includes mention of gratitude and thanksgiving over seventy-one times. Being grateful IN all is different than FOR all. Being grateful IN all means you are thankful for the good, bad, and the ugly. Grateful FOR all is only when and if something shows up in your life.

Seriously, it seems like God is asking too much, especially during times of great disappointments, tremendous losses, or unbearable heartaches. Life is hard enough and now we have to give thanks?! Comprehending this principle took me some time. I could not understand how to be grateful for my mother's death, a lost job, or a past of sexual abuse. The reality of giving thanks during these types of difficulties and challenges was an extreme challenge for me. You will have the same wrestling match I did as you work your way through these activities.

The intention is to think from possibility and not from the circumstance. We are not looking to be thankful FOR the difficulties; we are working to be grateful IN the new that comes from them. Unfortunately, many of us are programmed to look for what is wrong instead of what is right. We notice when we run into rude people, hit a traffic jam, get cut off by a crazy driver, lose a parking space, or lose a client. Being grateful IN everything starts with the small stuff. We can adjust our focus and look at the little things we can give thanks for in life.

Believing is Seeing

The pressing question is: can you give thanks and feel the gratitude with the desired outcome before it occurs? Can you imagine the desired result so vividly, you begin to live like it is already in the here and now? Are you willing to be so grateful for what you want and let go of the attachment to the outcome? If so, you are now ready to move into the next step, the concept of believing is seeing.

You are moving from cause and effect–the outside world determining your inside change– to causing an effect, changing your inner world to produce an external impact. Maintaining a state of gratitude will require you to use the conscious mind to practice gratitude. Using this technique communicates to both the SCM and the body that the event has already occurred. Your body must be convinced through your emotion that it is living the future experience while you are in the now.

In creating our new reality or state of being, we first have the desired thought and then feel about that thought, radically different from our old programming. As survivORs, it is vital that believing come first in our work and then seeing. You believe in something first to see it.

For example, if you believe in a successful outcome of what you will do, you will achieve it. Napoleon Hill, author of *Think and Grow Rich* said, "Whatever the mind can conceive and believe, it can achieve." He also said, "All success begins with definiteness of purpose, with a clear picture in your mind of precisely what you want from life." Do you realize he wrote these principles in 1937? The concept of thinking your life into reality has been around for a very long time. I think it is about time we catch up.

Denise has a remarkable ability to believe and then see. It's one of the mottos she lives by, believing is seeing. Denise has an unwavering faith that our minds, emotions, and feelings can be changed when focusing on them. She has made many changes in herself over the past three years and never doubts the power of her mind.

I want you to reject any past interpretations of your abuse. You get to write a new story about your past and imagine beyond what happened to you. Infinite intelligence or the electromagnetic field of possibility only responds to your every desire. As long as you bring your past into your present and future, you will attract into your life another event that will reproduce the same consequences and emotional responses. Every thought sends out a signal, combined with our emotions, and, in return, you will receive a person, place, or thing to match that emotional frequency.

Practicing Gratitude

To supercharge your power and practice the principle of believing is seeing, you must be grateful IN all. We have circled back to the implementation of these principles, the practice of gratitude. Here are a few ideas for you to incorporate into your daily lives:

- **Alphabet Gratitude.** Write or speak each letter of the alphabet and express one item you are grateful for under each letter.

- **Gratitude Journal**: Classic practice. I write at least ten things I am grateful for every night.

- **Gratitude Collage**: Create a collection of things you are grateful for in your life, now and in the future.

- **Gratitude Jar**: Design a jar that will hold your daily and weekly gratitudes. Simply put them on a strip of paper.

- **Circle of Gratitude**: This is an excellent activity for a family, group, or couple. Sit around in a circle and express what you are grateful for to each person.

- **Gratitude Artwork**: Paint, draw, scrapbook, needlepoint, or express gratitude in any other form of artistic expression.

- **Gratitude Flower**: Create flower petals of gratitude.

- **Gratitude Questions**: Ask yourself: 1) What touched me today? 2) Who or what inspired me today? 3) What made me smile today? 4) What's the best thing that happened today?

- **Gratitude Letter or Email / Gratitude Visit**: Write a hand-written letter to a person you are especially grateful to have in your life. Be detailed. Express all of their wonderful qualities.

- **Gratitude Partner:** Find someone to be a gratitude partner with and hold each other accountable.

- **Gratitude Walk:** I found that while I was walking my dogs or hiking, I could easily list the things I am grateful for in my life. You can also use the same concept as the game of I Spy. You can spy what you are grateful for and list them as you go.

- **Gratitude Prompts**: This is a fill-in-the-blanks activity. The goal is to identify at least three things in each category for which you are thankful.

The prompts include:

- I'm grateful for three things I hear, see, taste, touch, and smell:

  _____

- I'm grateful for three things about my body:

  _____

- I'm grateful for these three things I have overcome:

  _____

- I'm grateful for these three friends:

  _____

- I'm grateful for these three family members:

  _____

- I'm grateful for these three things in my home:

  _____

These are just a few examples of how you can implement gratitude in your everyday life, and you can make more up as you go. Get started right away, and you will fill up your life with gratitude.

Create a Vision

Create a Vision: I briefly talked about creating an image of your new empowering story. Creating a vision is an extended version of that, a statement of intent that you give to your life, your vision statement will immerse you in the "field of possibility." Your vision requires you to use your imagination to connect to the magnetic field to your desires through thoughts and emotions, and convince yourself that believing is seeing. The way to increase your flow of ideas and results is by developing the belief habit.

Your vision statement has several categories, such as health, wealth, relationships, volunteer work, physicality, career, spirituality, and other valued components of your life. You will design a vision to set up the foundation of your new state of being. You will begin each element with the statement: "I am so happy and grateful now that _____." You can make this a vision of tomorrow, next year, or three years from now.

Your vision statement is a potent activity to help you align with a bigger and better story in your life. When you create a vision statement, it is a request to the field of potential. The more you rehearse the life in your vision and how it feels, the more feedback you get from the field of possibility.

Ask for a sign from the field related to your specific desired outcomes. Making this request provides evidence that you are all in. You are demonstrating that you have embraced the concept of believing is seeing; you are willing to surrender to the unknown and trust in the results.

At first, look for the little signs and results. You will see a shift in your perception of things and conditions. Begin to notice the changes and monitor anything different, showing up in your life or thoughts.

AS IF Living: Live life AS IF everything you would love exists in the here and now. How does this look? Test drive the car you want. Tour the new home you admire. Shop in the stores you desire. Live AS IF all is now. In the book, *Through the Looking-Glass and What Alice Found There,* on which the movie *Alice in Wonderland* is based, there is a very enlightening conversation between Alice and the White Queen.

"It's a poor sort of memory that only works backward," the Queen remarked.

"What sort of things do YOU remember best?" Alice ventured to ask.

"Oh, things that happened the week after next," the Queen replied in a careless tone.

You have a valuable and skillful memory that works in both directions. Accept that if you decide and send a message to the field of possibility, you will create your reality. Do not be like Alice in the story. She doubted in this scene:

"There's no use trying," Alice said, "one CAN'T believe impossible things."

"I daresay you haven't had much practice," said the Queen. "When I was your age, I always did it for half an hour a day. Why, sometimes I've believed as many as six impossible things before breakfast."

Believe as many impossible things as you desire. Why? Nothing is impossible! We just need to get out of our way.

CHAPTER 10

Conquer Forgiveness

I need to warn you; I am going to drop the F-Bomb–Forgiveness! There was no more significant hurdle for me to face and overcome than the idea of forgiveness. People would say things to me about forgiveness, and I would shut down. I was NOT letting anyone off the hook! I was NOT going to forget. I was NOT going to be the *bigger person*.

I am sure you have heard this expression many times: unforgiveness is like drinking poison and hoping the other person dies. For a long time, I resisted accepting that to be even remotely true. After years of therapy, I came to the grim realization that as long as I didn't forgive, I was not over my abuse. AND–since I was not over it, that gave me permission to continue being mad, hurt, frustrated, resentful, and curse and rehearse the same thoughts and feelings around my life. I was stuck, and stuck stinks! It was inevitable that I needed to forgive. What I didn't expect was over the years, I would become a pro at forgiveness.

As they say, forgiveness is for you, not the other person. I know, like me, at that point, you might be starting this chapter with resistance. Here is what I learned: no one needs to know you forgave them. I did not go to my abusers and tell them I forgave them. I do not believe it is a necessary part of the process. Forgiveness is an inside job.

I believe forgiveness is an intellectual process. It is not a deeply emotional process, and I like to compare it to a unilateral business transaction. You get to decide on the fate of your transaction with your abuser. They do not get to vote or grant you permission. You are in control and will determine what is best for you.

I will walk you through the basics of forgiveness for when and if you participate. I highly recommend you give it a try. I never thought I would acknowledge it was the most significant part of my healing.

Forgiveness Does Not Mean Acceptance: Forgiveness does not mean you are now okay with your abuse or its destructive effects. You do not condone the behavior and actions; by no means do you agree or discount the abuse's impact. Forgiveness means you are releasing ownership of the abuse to the perpetrators. The process will allow you to stop carrying the burden of shame and guilt. As long as you hold the feelings around your abuse and do not forgive, you are fueling the fire, and to your mind, victimhood is still alive in your life. Forgiveness is putting the abuse back in its place.

Forgiveness Does Not Depend on the Other Person: This process only requires you and you alone. Many times, you do forgiveness work with people who are no longer living. It still works. You do not need your abuser(s) to be aware or present, and it is better if they are not. Trust me; more than likely, there won't be an apology. You are acknowledging the abuse and deciding to hand over the burden to the rightful owner. This power move allows you to stop being the focus of the abuse. It is your choice.

Forgiveness Does Not Discount the Past: The process of forgiving does not undo the damage of the abuse, nor does it dismiss, minimize, or eliminate the pain from the past. Instead, it releases the white-knuckle hold the emotions have on you. In turn, you will have the freedom to create a bigger and better state of being. You won't forget or pretend it didn't happen. Forgiveness is the way to accept and move on.

Forgiveness–The True F-Bomb: Forgiveness is a process that takes time and a willingness to do this for yourself. Forgiving your abuser can take a little bit of getting used to in your thoughts. Keep in mind you will run the victim program as long as you keep the fury alive. While you may not feel like a victim, the immense missing peace is the void of forgiveness.

For me, the greatest pain was from the lack of responsibility my abusers were willing to take. When we feel the other person has not fully grasped the painful consequences of their action, it can be incredibly hard to let it go. Forgiveness is a journey that only begins when you are ready to release all the feelings associated with being a victim.

Forgiveness is All About YOU: The power of forgiveness is profound. You get to decide what you are willing and not willing to carry. Forgiveness is an entirely selfish move; it is not what you do for someone else. The price you pay for not forgiving can be significant.

Don't let the lasting effects of your abuse occupy your system. The process is for you and only you. Free up some energy for greater peace, freedom, power, and life.

I acknowledge your work through these chapters, as you have realized and understood emotions and beliefs around your abuse, and listed consequences. I support you in using everything you have learned up to this point to move into forgiveness when you are ready. Your work will pay off, I promise. Scientists who have studied the brain and forgiveness found that when we think and successfully imagine forgiving someone, we show increased activity in our neural circuits responsible for empathy. This discovery tells us that empathy is connected to forgiveness and is an essential step in the process of healing.

Empathy is a significant aspect of forgiveness. When I arrived at this point in my process, I had zero feelings for my abusers. I reflected on the power of choice. For example, I did not choose my abuse, and I choose never to abuse anyone. Why should I look at them with empathy, I then concluded, as not everyone has the same potential? As I looked at my father's life, however, I began to gain a bit more insight into his motivations. I first had to imagine him as an innocent child, needing love and support. His mother was evil and overly controlling; his father abused him. He inherited the need for control, and his actions proved that. The abuse was a cry for power, which he didn't feel inside growing up. That's not an excuse, but rather an insight into his behavior.

Forgiveness begins with letting go of the anger and resentment. Here is an excellent method I used over and over again. In my mind, I would take my abusers to the depth of the ocean, the abyss. The first few times I took my father there, I left him to drown. After a few attempts, I finally started the work. I imagined my father first as a little kid. I knew as a child, he was in the image and likeness of God; he was not an evil man. When I pictured him at a soul level, there was not a single part of him that wanted to harm me. I saw the pain and suffering he endured. I would merely contemplate his life and awkward rise to power. I would also bring the burden of my feelings and the effects of the abuse with me, write them all down, and hand them over to my father. I would tell him that it is now his turn to carry the burden of his action. I was no longer going to allow him to have any power over me. Each time, he received a gift from me, which included my anger, hurt, regret, resentment, betrayal, and any other emotion that came up.

I repeated this over and over again. Each time I would go to the abyss, my anger began to lessen. My blame and shame slowly faded. I felt freer and had a great sense of peace. Feeling lighter and more alive, I actually found myself thanking my father for his absurd actions and horrific parenting skills. Eventually, I saw the meaning of my abuse. I would have regretted my life forever if I did not discover the purpose of the abuse I experienced.

Because I lived through my abusive childhood, I have saved thousands of kids from their abuse. Now I can see that writing this book is why I lived, to work with survivORs, and protect more children from perpetration. I choose to see the silver lining; otherwise, I would be bitter and hopeless in my life. We are not a victim to anyone or anything unless we choose to be.

Developing and shifting your state of mind or being requires trust in the process, patience, and commitment. Trust me when I say that the process will unfold. You do something enough times with the right intention, and the results don't happen sometimes. They happen all the time.

According to Dr. Joe Dispenza, *"True forgiveness is breaking the emotional charge and energetic bond to our painful past, whatever that might be. What you're left with instead is a memory, and a memory without the emotional charge is called wisdom."*

As you move into the process of forgiveness, you will find the emotional charge fades related to your memories. You find yourself feeling less and less activated by the memories. I began describing my abuse and dysfunctional upbringing as a gross inconvenience. I no longer have significant emotional responses to the past. Now the memories have faded, and I can't identify them around the events. The goal is to defuse the past and ignite the future.

Forgiveness is more of a rinse and repeat process. You will recall another trigger from your abuse; go back to the beginning and walk through the process. There will come a time when you will be shocked at the lack of response you have to the abuse, and, if you truly do the work, one day you will actually respond positively to your abuser. WHAT? Yes, I, too, was shocked when, after many trips to the abyss, I heard that my father was going to Disney World with his great-grandkids. The automatic thought that popped into my head was good for him; he loves those kids. I could not believe it!

The test for forgiveness is when you can move from resentment, anger, disdain, and hatred to a place of gratitude. My forgiveness work allowed me to have a very transparent relationship with my father. It also allowed me to reenter my family and work to break the cycle of abuse. While my father never heard the words "I forgive you" from my mouth, the greatest gift for me was forgiveness.

CHAPTER 11

Earned Peace

I hope you are so addicted to the thought of an *OR* life that you are obsessed with who you are becoming and nothing else at this point in the book. Peace will become a full-time job for you, as earning peace is about staying aware, awake, alert, and alive. Peace requires living in the present moment by creating the future now. Pull the rearview mirror off and see the view through the windshield. A clue is in the size of each: the bigger perspective is out the front, into the future. The rearview is the small view, and that's what it is: PAST! Now, it is time for peace.

Let's start with peace of mind. The most crucial step is to surrender. Yikes! That means we must allow a power more incredible and loving than us to take the wheel; it is an acquired habit of thinking! After years and years of work, this remains my constant nemesis. I find I must wrestle with the old belief that nothing will happen if I am not in control.

The only limit to our peace and success is our thinking, and peace of mind begins with fully understanding that you alone cannot cause a result in your life without the quantum field of infinite possibility. More than likely, the greatest struggle in creating your desires is in the how. The HOW, as you have previously read, is none of your business. Therefore, you get to partner with the field of possibility beyond yourself and delight in the unexpected.

Let's create a greater state of peace by surrendering and letting go, which means setting aside your ego and expectation for a specific outcome. Just as we practice gratitude and envision a new future before we can see it, creating peace requires you to trust in an unexpected result produced by this more expanded power. You don't know what you don't know until you know it!

To accomplish this newfound attitude, you must live in the possibility and feel it.

Begin to feel freedom, joy, fun, calm, or a state of bliss to match the outcome you desire. This communication to the stream of possibility demonstrates you accept and welcome the result as a reality. Living as if all is real and more is coming, this greater force or stream of infinite possibility can do what it does best. You will experience a more orderly life and more outstanding results based on your future thinking, rather than reactive living. Each day, live life as if your

problems are solved, and your greatest desires are on their way to you. Living in the result and knowing without a doubt, there is nothing to worry about, long for, or miss brings great peace of mind.

Surrender Control

Here is a practical method to allow yourself to surrender and let go of the need for control.

Step 1: Find a quiet place for you to be alone. Lock the door to prevent any access to the room. You want to be free to feel safe. Determine the amount of time you would like to spend on this exercise. I like to give myself a maximum of twenty minutes. Others allow for an hour or more. Decide and commit to experimenting with surrendering for the time allotted.

Step 2: Next, bring to mind the current limitations you have and what you want to change about yourself. Define the emotion and reaction you would like to release.

Step 3: Begin a conversation with your higher power, and outwardly state the emotion you are releasing. This declaration will command your mind and body to release the hold these emotions have on you. You may want to see the emotion or situation in a giant bubble rising up and away. I encourage you to use any means of visualization to release and let go of this part of your past.

Step 4: Finally, express gratitude to this higher mind and power for resolving the situation. Confidently, know that the power greater than you has taken this over this situation, and the perfect solution is on its way. You do not need to know how or when; know all is perfect.

Keep in mind what you mentally rehearse and what you physically experience in this exercise creates the result on a neurological level. In only a matter of time, desire becomes a reality.

Earned peace is obtained by continually reminding yourself to stay conscious throughout your day. Train yourself to be aware of any limiting thoughts or behaviors. I find the best way to stop my thinking's downward spiral immediately is to say, "STOP." I say it to myself or out loud. I follow up with, "Oh no, this is not a good time. I will schedule time with you later." Next, go to the surrender exercise and let go of the old program. You will eventually find the word STOP will be the most potent and reasonable voice in your head.

I would love to say this always works. While it is not fail-proof, it helps you get a jumpstart on the downward trajectory. You will find words that redirect your thinking. The idea is to repeatedly interrupt the old programs and weaken the strength of the past. The goal is to be awake and have conscious control of your thoughts and feelings. No longer will you be a victim of your knee-jerk emotional reactions. The past is full of your limited ways of thinking and feeling.

I have always owned and loved dogs, and I decided to train every dog I owned to act like humans. People repeatedly told me, dogs can't reason; however, every dog I had could make their own decisions. I would ask any of my dogs a multiple-choice question, and they would decide their best option. I am not kidding. People would witness the reasoning power of my dogs and be astounded. My dogs all trusted and surrendered to the safety of my care. I gave them clear limits and boundaries, which allowed them to trust.

When my dogs and I were hiking and someone was coming, I would say, "Place." Each dog would immediately find something higher than ground level, jump up, and let others pass by. They would patiently sit until released. "Place" was an indication to them that a new path or action was required. STOP is an indication to the mind it's time for a new direction.

There are so many triggers and stimuli causing you to stray into an old memory or associated connection. You will find yourself moving away from the new thought patterns into the old, predictable desires where you think, act, feel, and create the same old reality. Your old emotions and thoughts represent a low frequency of energy that puts your body into action. So, earning peace is consistently being conscious and willing to change your thoughts before making it to the body. You will be so awake you notice and redirect immediately to the new state of being. You can use STOP, KNOCK IT OFF, or PLACE to interrupt the thoughts taking you away from your desired *OR* life.

The mind notifies the body to act. To have peace of mind and body, you must rehearse and memorize your new life. Rose Tremain says, *"Life is not a dress rehearsal."* I say, until you have an audience, rehearse all you can. Let me explore this idea. As the director, you must have the vision and provide the actors and stagehands (known as higher power and molecules) with their roles. If you recall, thoughts that fire together wire together. Keep rehearsing the scene of life in your mind, and everything will conspire to be on your side. Good or bad, the thoughts you fire will wire the results by magnetizing your thoughts and emotions. Life is not a dress rehearsal, so you put on a great show right up to the moment of your last breath.

Here are a few questions to help you move into thinking and acting in your chosen way:

- How would I love to be confident?
- If I was confident, how would I think?
- What thoughts enhance my certainty?
- What is my new attitude or mantra?
- How do I perceive myself?
- What would I say to myself if I was this person?
- In my certainty, how would I act?
- In my certainty, what would I do?
- Who would I do it with or not?
- How do I see myself walking in the world?
- How would I communicate in this new expression of self?
- What would I feel?
- Would I take more *risks*?
- Would I step out of my comfort zone?
- What more can I create?

Rehearsing your new way of certainty requires knowing how you will think, act, and feel. You are stepping into the creative process. Use your imagination and go beyond your ordinary thinking. Remember to suspend the need to know HOW. You cannot force your answers and control the outcome of your vision.

To design your best self, ask:

- What is the most magnificent version of myself?
- What would it be like to be this person?
- Who do I admire, and how do/did they act?
- What would it be like to think, feel, and act like him/her?
- What would my life look like if I were that person?
- What would I say to myself if I were this person?
- What would others say to or about me?

Rehearse and memorize your new and most fabulous self. Memorize your every thought and feeling to create a unique and improved internal order. Think further than your current circumstances and build peace of mind and body. When your thoughts and actions match your intentions, you can be sure the results are on their way to you. You are no longer controlled by your environment or reacting to your circumstance. You have created the exact opposite. You are in charge and moving life into the reality you desire. NOW, you are relieved of your past and no longer merely surviving–you are living beyond what happened to you.

Earned Success

It is inevitable when one finds peace, success follows. It can't NOT! No matter your definition of success, you will find the things you desire most will fall into your lap. The struggle and effort for more will lessen, and you will begin to understand the magic that results from peace of mind.

My vision is to send you on your way to massive success when you conclude reading this book. I know only too well that abuse is the "gift that keeps on giving." One layer of your abuse gives way to the next one in need of healing. First and foremost, accept this journey as lifelong; the beauty is that the effort required becomes far less, and the expansive growth far more.

Success for me is living in peace. I have experienced this peace after years and years of driving and striving to fill the void. It took a long time to realize NOTHING IS MISSING. There was no missing peace or piece. I was attempting to find what was there all along, buried by all the past patterns and experiences. This revelation is excellent news! If nothing is missing, then we need to reveal it within ourselves. Remember that success of any kind follows peace. How you experience a feeling of peace and fulfillment is to breathe. Yes, breathing.

A more recent practice I have been using is the HeartMath system.

(https://store.heartmath.com/heartmath-experience/)

The HeartMath system empowers people to self-regulate their emotions and behaviors to reduce stress, increase resilience, and unlock their natural intuitive guidance for making more effective choices. This method enables people to break through to increased personal balance, creativity, insight, and health. HeartMath bases learning programs and the emWave® and Inner Balance™ self-regulation technology on over 29 years of scientific research on the psychophysiology of stress, resilience, and the interactions between the heart and brain.

Without diving too deep into the system, I want to give you my quick overview. There are emotions, good and bad. Bad because you feel constriction and resistance which causes incoherence. Good emotions result in an opening or freeing feeling which creates coherence. When measured, the bad emotions produce an erratic patterned heartbeat; good emotions make a nice, smooth, flowing wave. How do you maintain a coherent heart rhythm? Breathe. Understanding the role of breathing is vital. Many times we breathe only enough to stay alive when we are in stressful situations. Breath is the primary cure for all that ails us. Complete focus on our breathing can develop patterns of ease and flow in our mind and body.

I use a HeartMath Monitor. This link is for their newest version:

https://www.heartmath.org/store/products/inner-balance/

Coherent heart rhythm is when you experience uplifting emotions such as gratitude, joy, affection, care, appreciation, and love.

Your heart rhythm pattern becomes highly ordered and smooth. When you're coherent/ when you're breathing coherently, coupled with imaging your deepest desires, will bring about even greater coherence and result in your mind and body's new wiring. Practice breathing every day. Be aware of your thoughts and emotions. This conscious awareness works for all situations and allows you to feel a sense of confidence, power, and peace.

What does this mean to you? Pay attention! Notice your breathing and always know why you do what you do. If you are out of coherence, stressed, pressured, or anxious, stop and breathe. Do not ever again muscle through life and tasks. Be present, be grateful, and be committed. PEACE be with you, created by you, and for only you!

CHAPTER 12

OR Living

*L*iving an *OR* life is about taking back your power. Today, you get to decide how to live. Sometimes the old you will take you down a path unaligned with your *OR* life.

Warning: you might outgrow, expand beyond, or leave some people behind. I have found that I have had to say goodbye to people that didn't serve me over the years. I discovered people wanted me to be the me they knew; the me based on my past, not my truth. What is your truth? What are you here to do? Who are you here to be? Why aren't you already that?

You have passed by your true desires and expressions for far too long. I know I did. I was held hostage by my past, I felt shame for wanting more, and I stayed in relationships too long for the wrong reasons. I settled and put up with such lack. Never again. I command an *OR* life.

How does your *OR* life look? An *OR* life is one you design free from the past. It is a life you want to live, an experience that's exciting, inspirational, and stimulating. *OR* living means you must suspend the need to know how and embrace the why.

Please continue to rewire the mind to a new and improved normal. This commitment requires you to give up the need for control and trust; there is a field of infinite possibility seeking to bring you what you command. The quantum field of possibility is at your service, waiting for you to think, feel, and ask.

Many times people will ask for help in fixing the past, rather than designing the future. That's asking the wrong question. Real control is in embracing the connection between thinking, feeling, and asking for what you desire. Refrain from praying, asking, or begging for things to go away or change. Ask for precisely what you want and feel into it. Your focus determines the extent to which you create or control your world.

I have spent years creating a new me for a new life. I trust that my desire to share my story, life, and journey has helped you find your power. In your power, you can do anything. Whether you want that new job, business, partner, wealth, health, or more, it is solely up to you.

Many won't do it. I know I have been lazy over the years, occasionally falling victim to my past. I can find myself in the middle of a "pity party." Trust me; we have reasons to feel sorry for ourselves.

The problem is no one cares. I mean, there is caring, except there is not a soul on this earth that can change our lives except us. You will find every day that something will try to pull you away from your path. The world will not slow down for you to master the new way of thinking and being. Heck, most of the time, you won't slow down either!

Have I provided enough shortcuts and compelling information to inspire you to dive into the deep end and learn how to swim? That is my hope for you. I can attest to the fact that the information and techniques I have provided work. I have lived them, as have thousands who engage in my *Revealing the Missing PEACE* program.

Decide to be at peace. No one or nothing can make you feel a sense of peace. Do not rely on others to make your world a better place. Find beautiful things in your life that make you feel a sense of peace. Climb a mountain, jump in a lake, get a massage, hug a puppy, paint a picture, ride a bike, hike, have sex, high-five a stranger, do random acts of kindness, take a nap, go to church, don't go to church, watch a movie, call in sick, buy yourself something, or buy me something!!! What makes you feel at peace? If you do not know, FIND SOMETHING!! No more letting others cut to the front of your line. You are Number One in your life and deserve to be first.

There is a saying: *"You can live ninety years or live one year ninety times."* That is *Groundhog Day* living. Bill Murray didn't like it, and you shouldn't either. Living the same life over and over again is giving power to your past. The power of the past is strong and habitual. Habits take a while to create. Get so committed to your new and improved way of thinking that nothing stops you. There will be days you fall, get back up, dust yourself off, and go for it. The past is history; the future is yours to create, with no more reruns in your life. Choose your thoughts and feelings carefully in everything you do. Be sure to interrupt thoughts that do not serve you. Change them at the moment to what you want to create at that moment to shape your future. Live your *OR* life, and make no apologies.

What More to Say?

First and foremost, I want to extend my appreciation for you engaging in this work with me. I have been on a mission to change the way survivors live. My extensive work taking trauma victims on a journey to surviv*OR*ship and beyond has given me a unique perspective. I have done my best to communicate these insights throughout the book. There are too many who have suffered at the hands of their perpetrators. What infuriates me is how they settle for a life unexpressed. My heart breaks every time I hear, "I don't need to deal with it," or "I have just moved on from it." NO ONE needs to settle for a less than full *OR* life. You can be a victim, survive–*OR*. You have decided to *OR* live life fully by embracing what you deserve and desire.

The power of your past will do everything to pull you down. Stand strong, be firm, and know you can live beyond what they told you, what they said about you, and what happened to you. You have the tools.

To be a surviv*OR* is to be who you want to be precisely in the way you want to be that person. You get to be your successful, expressive, determined, unapologetic, direct, assertive, sexual, sensual, shame-free, guilt-free, powerful SELF!!!

Stand UP! Speak UP! Play Full Out in an *OR* life.

Chapter 1

Abuse data - For abuse data, visit http://www.d2l.org/wp-content/uploads/2017/01/all_statistics_20150619.pdf to learn more.

comparanoia™. Davide Di Giorgio.

"Dissociative Disorders." NAMI (National Alliance On Mental Health). https://www.nami.org/About-Mental-Illness/Mental-Health-Conditions/Dissociative-Disorders

Nobel Prize® is a registered trademark of the Nobel Foundation. The Nobel Peace Prize is one of several Nobel Prizes awarded by the Nobel Foundation.

Oxy.IR, a form of the drug Oxycodone, which is a potent opioid drug.

The Power and Control Wheel and Equality Wheel were developed by the Domestic Abuse Intervention Program (DAIP) in 1984 in Duluth, MN. It is produced and distributed by the National Center for Domestic and Sexual Violence.

Chapter 2

"Do Not Let the Behavior of Others Destroy Your Inner Peace. - Dalai Lama." Quotes Pedia, April 9, 2020. https://www.quotespedia.org/authors/d/dalai-lama/do-not-let-the-behavior-of-others-destroy-your-inner-peace-dalai-lama/.

EMDR is a trademark of E.M.D.R. Institute, Inc.

"Mahatma Gandhi Quote: 'Outward Peace Is Useless without Inner Peace.'." Quotefancy.

https://quotefancy.com/quote/858584/Mahatma-Gandhi-Outward-Peace-is-useless-without-inner-Peace.
Petrie, Daniel, director. Sybil. NBC, 1976.

"Quote by Lao Tzu." Goodreads.
https://www.goodreads.com/quotes/523350-if-you-are-depressed-you-are-living-in-the-past.

"Wayne W. Dyer Quotes." Notable Quotes
http://www.notable-quotes.com/d/dyer_wayne_w.html.
What Is PSYCH-K® is a trademark of the Myrddin Corporation.

Chapter 3

Quote: Harkleroad, Jenny. "You Are Good Enough." Balanced You - Mind Reprogramming Facilitation - San Diego, CA, April 6, 2018.
https://balancedyou.org/you-are-good-enough/.

of the Cross, John, and Peers, E. Allison (translator), "The Dark Night of the Soul (La Noche Oscura del Alma)", May 9, 2003, Dover Publications (first published 1584).

Chapter 4

AMAC: https://www.amazon.com/Adults-Molested-As-Children-Survivors/dp/1884444032
YMCA is the trademark of YMCA of the USA.

Chapter 5

"Fight or Flight" is a concept first described by Walter Bradford Cannon.

Chapter 6

Clance, Dr. Pauline R. and Suzanne A. Imes. "The Imposter Phenomenon in High Achieving Women: Dynamics and Therapeutic Intervention." *Psychotherapy Theory, Research and Practice* 15.3 (1978)

Proctor, Bob. "EVERYTHING Starts With a Decision." Proctor Gallagher Institute, July 16, 2020. https://www.proctorgallagherinstitute.com/tips-and-tools/decision-making.

"Quote by Anais Nin." Goodreads.
https://www.goodreads.com/quotes/348178-shame-is-the-lie-someone-told-you-about-yourself

"Quote by Erma Bombeck." Goodreads.
https://www.goodreads.com/quotes/592805-guilt-the-gift-that-keeps-on-giving

"Quote by Sigmund Freud." Goodreads.
https://www.goodreads.com/quotes/422467-unexpressed-emotions-will-never-die-they-are-buried-alive-and

Williams, Carol J. "The Unwanted Children: Casualties Left by a
Tyrant: Romania: Abandoned Youngsters Fill Orphanages That Resemble Warehouses.
Aid Does Not Always Reach Them." Los Angeles Times. Los Angeles Times, December
10, 1990. https://www.latimes.com/archives/la-xpm-1990-12-10-mn-4673-story.html.

Chapter 7

Alcoholics Anonymous is a trademark of Alcoholics Anonymous World Services, Inc.

Bactine is a trademark of Wellspring Pharmaceutical Corporation.

Beck, Martha. "You've Spot It, You've Got It." O, The Oprah
Magazine, July 2004.
https://www.oprah.com/spirit/martha-beck-you-spot-it-youve-got-it/all

Murphy's Law, which says "anything that can go wrong will go wrong," was coined by
Air Force engineer Captain Edward Aloysius Murphy Jr. http://www.murphys-laws.com/murphy/murphy-true.html

Narcotics Anonymous is a trademark of Narcotics Anonymous World Services, Inc.

Chapter 8

Etch a Sketch is a Trademark of Spin Master LTD. https://trademarks.justia.com/721/10/etch-a-72110281.html.

Hendricks, Gay. The Big Leap. New York: HarperCollins, 2009.

Jacobs-Kayam, Angi, Lev-Wiesel, Rachel. "In Limbo: Time Perspective and Memory Deficit Among Female Survivors of Sexual Abuse." *Frontiers in Psychology*, vol. 10 (April 2019): 912, https://doi.org/10.3389/fpsyg.2019.00912

Kershner, Irvin, and Lucas, George. 1980. *The Empire Strikes Back*, United States: Twentieth Century-Fox Film Corporation. "Nelson Mandela Quote." AZQuotes. http://azquotes.com/quote/185315.

Pavlov, Ivan. 1849-1936, Nobel Prize in Physiology or Medicine (1904)

"Quote by Henry Ford." Goodreads. https://www.goodreads.com/quotes/7518455-whether-you-think-you-can-or-think-you-can-t-you

Ramis, Harold. 1993. *Groundhog Day*. United States: Columbia Pictures

Chapter 9

Carroll, Lewis. Through the Looking-Glass and What Alice Found There. New York: Macmillan Publishers, 1871.

Dispenza, Dr. Joe. Becoming Supernatural: How Common People *Are Doing The Uncommon*. California: Hay House Inc., 2017

Fersen, Eugene. Science of Being. New York: Lightbearers Publishing, LLC: 2013. https://www.encyclopedia.com/humanities/dictionaries-thesauruses-pictures-and-press-releases/pushmi-pullyu

Gamblers Anonymous (Gam-Anon) is a trademark of the Gam-Anon International Service Office, Inc.
Definition of Insanity: https://www.cornerstoneofrecovery.com/discovering-the-east-tennessee-ties-to-the-definition-of-insanity/

Geronimi, Clyde, Luske, Hamilton, and Jackson, Wilfred. 1951.
Alice in Wonderland. United States: Walt Disney Productions.

Hill, Napoleon. Think and Grow Rich. Connecticut: The Ralston Society, 1937. Overeaters Anonymous is a trademark of OA, Inc.

"Pushmi-Pullyu." Encyclopedia.com https://www.encyclopedia.com/humanities/dictionaries-thesauruses-pictures-and-press-releases/pushmi-pullyu

The term "Oscars" is a trademark of The Academy of Motion Pictures Arts and Sciences. "Quote by Narcotics Anonymous." Goodreads. https://www.goodreads.com/quotes/5543-insanity-is-doing-the-same-thing-over-and-over-again

Quantum Mechanics of the Law of Attraction: https://markahaughtonquantumvibrationalnumbers.com/quantum-mechanics-of-the-law-of-attraction/

Chapter 10

Dispenza, Dr. Joe. "Forgiving the Past to Create the Future." Dr. Joe Dispenza's Blog, December 20, 2019. https://blog.drjoedispenza.com/blog/change/forgiving-the-past-to-create-the-future.

Chapter 11

emWave® is a breath pacer that is a trademark of Quantum Intech, Inc. Inner Balance™ is a self-regulation sensor that is is a trademark of Quantum Intech, Inc.

"The Heartmath Experience." Heartmath. https://www.heartmath.com/experience/

"Quote by Rose Tremain." Goodreads. https://www.goodreads.com/quotes/165342-life-is-not-a-dress-rehearsal.

Chapter 12

Acknowledgements

About Jane M Powers

*R*ecognized for her ability to navigate and heal the most challenging circumstances, Jane M Powers is an award-winning international speaker, trainer, and sought-after life and business strategist.

Her dedication in guiding trauma surviv*OR*s to emerge victorious over their past and into an unstoppable future has deemed her the quintessential go-to expert. Jane is fully committed to you, creating deep, genuine healing to live a remarkable life that matters, just as she has through the healing of her abuse. She knows how to reveal the missing peace; you must find your voice; in your voice is your power.

Jane is from the Chicagoland area and now lives in the searing desert of Phoenix, AZ. She is an avid outdoors adventurer and loves to be in nature. Her motto, "If it ain't fun, I'm Done!"

She has used her straightforward, big-hearted style to guide thousands to Speak with Confidence and Sell with Authority during her expansive career.

She has decades of successful speaking, training, and coaching under her belt. Perhaps the most important of her real-life experiences are the founding and running of three multi-million-dollar businesses. Jane appreciates that success is truly about the power of your VOICE. She brings you everything you need to ensure a competitive edge in your healing.

About Denise M Powers

*C*herished by many for her brilliance, kindness, and commitment to growth, Denise M Powers has inspired many to be their best self. Whether teaching fourth and fifth graders or rubbing elbows with the likes of Tom Hanks, Ron Howard, and other accomplished directors,

Denise's influence in the world is undeniable. She has affected others to increase their authenticity and live a wholly shameless life. Her transformation through the SurvivOR Method has been nothing shy of amazing.

Denise is a native Arizonan and mother of two. She has successfully managed and scaled a multi-million-dollar business. Her signature success is based on one simple principle, be YOU without compromising others in your quest for success.

Denise earned her MA in Education from Arizona State University and her BS in Business Management from the University of Phoenix.

The unrelenting commitment Denise displays in her quest for her healing, and the support of others is immeasurable. She has dedicated her life to living full out with bold confidence and leading others to do the same. Make no mistake; she is not just another pretty face.

Photos by Emily Aspell – Every Love Photography –
https://facebook.com/everlovephotography.com

For additional information, support and videos go to:
www.revealingthemissingpeace.com

We invite you to leave a review of our book:

Goodreads
Amazon
Other Book Retailers

Other books by
Jane M Powers

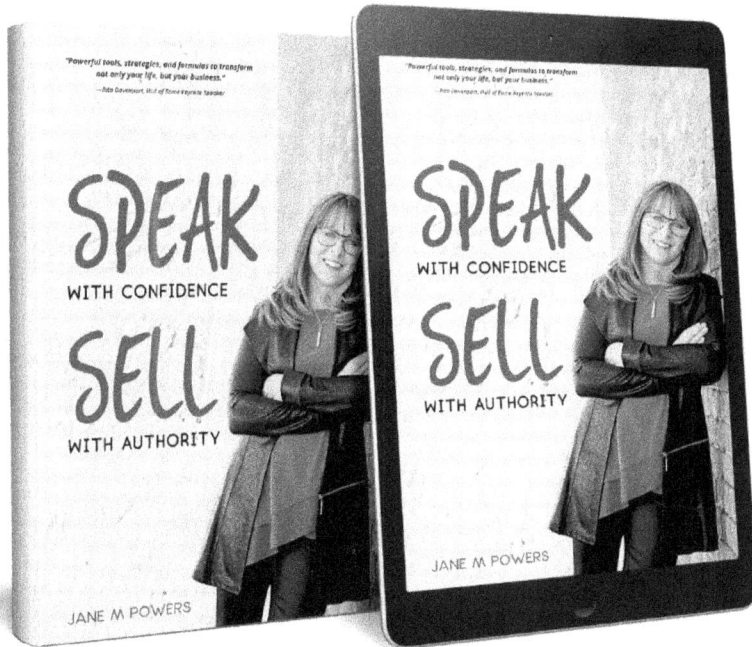

https://amzn.to/3nhGW0o

www.ingramcontent.com/pod-product-compliance
Lightning Source LLC
Chambersburg PA
CBHW081641040426
42449CB00015B/3407